THE
BALANCE THEORY

the kind press

NATASHA PICCOLO

THE
BALANCE
THEORY

Copyright © 2022 Natasha Piccolo
First published by the kind press, 2022

All rights reserved. No part of this book may be reproduced, stored in a retrieval system or transmitted in any form or by any means, electronic, mechanical photocopying, recording, or otherwise, without written permission from the author and publisher.

This publication contains the opinions and ideas of its author. It is intended to provide helpful and informative material on the subjects addressed in the publication. While the publisher and author have used their best efforts in preparing this book, the material in this book is of the nature of general comment only. It is sold with the understanding that the author and publisher are not engaged in rendering medical advice or any other kind of personal professional service in the book. In the event that you use any of the information in this book for yourself, the author and the publisher assume no responsibility for your actions.

Cover Design: Mila Book Covers
Internal design: Nicola Matthews, Nikki jane Design
Edited by Georgia Jordan

Cataloguing-in-Publication entry is available from the National Library Australia.

ISBN: 978-0-6451392-3-5
ISBN: 978-0-6451392-4-2 (ebook)

For my Travelling Partners. You know who you are.

Acknowledgement to Country

The author wishes to acknowledge the Cabrogal people of the Darug Nation as Traditional Owners of Country where this book was written. The author pays respects to Aboriginal and Torres Strait Islander people from all Nations as the Traditional custodians and storytellers throughout the land. The author pays respect to Elders past, present and emerging and acknowledges that sovereignty was never ceded.

Disclaimer

The client names used in this story are pseudonyms to ensure client confidentiality and to protect privacy.
The use of all other names used in this book was consented to. The author acknowledges the integrity of each individual who has given permission to have their story shared in this work.

Trigger warning

This book discusses topics such as depression, anxiety, mental illness, loss, grief and trauma. Should this book trigger any undesirable feelings for you, my dear reader, please know you can seek help immediately. You are not alone.

Lifeline: 13 11 14

CONTENTS

The Divine Nine

About your author vxii

Prologue xix

Chapter 1
The Birth of The Balance Theory 1
The Lesson: This too shall pass.

Chapter 2
The Call to Homeostasis—Balance in the Body 23
The Lesson: The Universe is observed at all levels of life.
There is a Universally guided intelligence system.

Chapter 3
Balance of 'the Mind' 49
The Lesson: The mind is the gateway.

Chapter 4
How We 'Human' 83
The Lesson: Authenticity is the universal motivator.

Chapter 5
The Divine Dance 103
The Lesson: Balanced bipolarities create space for truth.

Chapter 6
Travelling Partners 129
The Lesson: Our connections prepare us for the ultimate surrender.

Chapter 7
Navigating Adversity 159
The Lesson: A life without adversity is a life imbalanced.

Chapter 8
Observable Reality 185
The Lesson: A cellular inhale is a collective exhale.

Chapter 9
Kismet Connection 209
The Lesson: Connection to Self, Other and the world is ultimately kismet. Balance is a divine Universal act.

Notes 231
Acknowledgements 233
About the Author 239

What The Balance Theory is not

My brain lives in a harmonious dichotomy.
Creativity and science.
They go hand in hand.
Hemisphere by hemisphere.
And as a result,
I have to respect the place of both.
Whilst I'm (professionally) a scientist, I am first and foremost a thinker.
And thinkers aren't bound by laws, constants or the need to 'prove' anything necessarily.
The Balance Theory is not about physical observation in the traditional sense.
It's about observation of the mind;
Of the spirit.
And therefore doesn't exist on the human plane alone.
The Balance Theory operates in a different space to science.
Therefore, in my mind, it coexists—
With science,
And whatever else is out there.
Observable.
Hidden.
Real.
Imagined.

Hello, curious reader.

Welcome to *The Balance Theory*.

The book in your hands is a collection of downloads offered through me, Natasha Piccolo, over the course of the last ten years.

Well, really, the process has probably occurred my entire life, but the past decade, these sacred learnings channelled into one complete body of work. It has asked to be shared with you all. So here we are.

The Balance Theory is for everyone, no matter what you believe about our place and purpose here.

So, I pose to you, what if all the Universe wanted was to experience balance? What if we could simplify our existence to just that?

Non-attachment.

Then, in our suffering, we no longer have to suffer.

It's not about surrendering our power to the gods and spiritually bypassing our unresolved trauma and emotional turmoil. Instead, could it be that we are co-creating this universal *balance system* in our outer world? Could it be that when we die, we pass energetically into the next plane, the next realm, the next aether, for the sake of balancing energy elsewhere?

What if that's all it really was?

A peaceful take on death sure makes for a peaceful take of life, don't you think?

Clinically, I have witnessed universal systems of balance time and time again. As a clinical speech-language pathologist, both my work and my study have revealed, through many facets, the notion of balance being played on multiple levels. From human cell biology to organ systems, and then, the human body operating as a holistic, harmonious unit.

These body systems become a person.

This person then takes their intelligent state of being and in a desperate, evolutionary bid, attempts to connect with Other—another human, a fellow sentient being. A relationship goes through ups and downs all in an attempt to touch balance. Communication is the bridge, the barometer by which we measure balance.

At this stage, The Balance Theory is revealing to us now that energetic interplay exists truly, both inside and outside of oneself. Likely, defying the space-time continuum. We dance with this idea even more when we introduce the idea of the *Travelling Partner* (in Chapter 6), a person with whom we connect so strongly, it exceeds all human reasoning.

Perhaps we recognise this soul across lifetimes, and so our human experience with this person feels so much more than that.

The Balance Theory doesn't belong to me—it comes through me for us.

For you.

For me.

For our communities and beyond.

Each chapter, we will walk through the ways in which this ideology presents itself on multiple levels—from the cellular to the cosmic, and back again.

Full circle.

Union.

Yin.

Yang.

Balance.

About your author

So, who am I?

To introduce myself, my name is Natasha Piccolo. I play many roles in my day-to-day life, but to sum up, my life is all about being both the listener and the speaker. The space holder. I once described my life's purpose as being 'the people's person'. It rings true for me on a daily basis.

I have a wide circle of friends and a larger-than-life family who tend to come to me for 'a quick chat'. This can turn into hours. A beautiful way to pass time with those I love. Communication—both verbal and non-verbal—is the essential piece of my mission.

Professionally, I am a communication soundboard. Quite literally—first and foremost as a clinical speech pathologist working with children, adults and their families. This line of work led me to complete a Diploma of Life Coaching so that I could continue to expand the scope of my practice.

I've always been drawn to life's polarities. The astrologically inclined would say that this is the Gemini in me. The deepest understanding of light and dark for me came through the manifestation of a severe clinical depression and anxiety disorder at the age of twenty. I came full circle with my own mental health journey by my twenty-eighth birthday—I was equal parts medically and psychologically healed. To top it off, I had a sprinkle of full-moon cleanses, meditations and mantras to boot. The healing I experienced over the course of my mental health journey was a *balanced* mix of both Eastern and Western philosophies of 'wellness'.

Throughout my darkest moments, I intuitively knew that what I was experiencing held a higher purpose. That knowing got me through my most challenging days.

The Balance Theory is a collection of my deepest and most profound learnings over the past decade. It revealed itself as a sacred set of teachings, neatly boxed and delivered in mysterious packaging.

The name of the teachings came to me in a meditation as *The Divine Nine*.

Nine universal life lessons in the name of *balance.*

Prologue

We commence this earthside journey in 2011. The end of the year: 30 December. The day my dear friend Dylan passed away.

Nineteen years of love and laughs ended abruptly on that fateful day—he had fallen asleep behind the wheel and collided with a tree. In a split second, Dylan's earthly existence ended.

And with his death, I got a crack into true perspective.

Blood running cold, mouth unable to close from the shock, I slammed my bedroom door—naively, demanding the answers.

'Universe, just tell me why! Please, for my own sanity. Why, at nineteen years old, is it fair to have your life and everything of importance just *end*?'

And did the Universe respond?

Short answer: Yes. Yes it did.

Hard, fast, intense ... crazy.

But not without a huge serving of 'life lessons', and a bit of pain and truth as the two tantalising side dishes.

I spent the better part of the next two weeks, during January 2012, scribbling thoughts, pictures and images that revealed themselves as an odd set of universal truths, often scrawled on the back of prescription papers as I dispensed pharmacy medication over twelve-hour shifts that summer. The name came to me instantaneously.

The Balance Theory.

The voice whispered: *All the Universe is trying to achieve is balance. That is the experience. The time and space felt in this experience is our direct experience of 'life'.*

Simple, isn't it?

The Balance Theory is a concept that asks you to perceive *everything* that has ever existed as moving energy. It's observable by scientific method. It's consistent with esoteric principles of *afterlife* and *past lives* and all of the lives that you could be experiencing beyond what is tangible in the 3D plane, if that feels true for you.

It just *is*.

The series of 'downloads' that I received that year, and in the years to come, shaped into a set of 'truths'—although they had not been acknowledged in that way at the time. I was yet to embody the lessons. They were first a messed-up collection of thoughts and feelings amassed into numerous journals and iPhone notes over ten years. They kept me sane and comforted through some of the most testing moments of my life—through grief and depression and anxiety and panic attacks and OCD … the beautiful concoction of mental illness that taunted me throughout my early twenties.

Like many before me, it was travelling—literally travelling and getting out of my comfort zone—that was the space in which I learned the most about myself in such a short, compact period of time. I remember having a giggle to myself when

I witnessed a fellow traveller whip out *The Secret* while on a bus somewhere between Amsterdam and Prague. At the time, my scientifically indoctrinated mind blocked anything that entertained the idea of anything outside of the parameters of human cell biology—this was during peak university days, after all. You can imagine the cognitive dissonance that was running through my very logical and put-together left brain at the time. I was completely burdened by the downloads that were just begging to be acknowledged ...

The experience of mental illness was formally diagnosed for me in April of 2011—eight months before Dylan tragically lost his life. *The Balance Theory* was in its infancy before that level of loss was ever felt. I was just a young woman in her early twenties, attempting to articulate her racing mind and make sense of the world beyond her own mental mess. The concept accelerated at full force when the Universe offered the 'last straw' in the form of taking Dylan's life.

Meanwhile, my university study was in full swing. Days and nights soon became flooded with diagrams, figures, graphs and sketches itemising the inner workings of human neuropsychology and communication theory as I grew further into my role as a student of clinical speech pathology. And with a degree that was so science heavy and evidence based—the opposite started to happen. My questioning for life outside of 'life' only deepened.

Curiosity—deepened.

Confusion—deepened even more so, to say the least.

It was then that Universe, Source, God, whoever and I

needed to have a conversation.

This communication is channelled now—for you, the reader—in the chapters that follow.

Looking back on those early writings now, the glimpses of Universal insight were beginning to reveal themselves—without any understanding outside of my own context. The world of yoga, meditation, Abraham Hicks teachings, crystals, chakras, etc. was not even in my (conscious) field at the time …

But I believed in something—the experience of mental illness was so tremendously dark that believing in something else was the only way to accept that human life really was worth the 'living'.

So I believed. I had no choice. In what? I wasn't sure. But I had (a new-found) faith.

CHAPTER 1
The Birth of The Balance Theory

The Lesson: This too shall pass.

March 2011: My quarter-life crisis

I'm writing this down because I feel like I need to. Right now. At this inconvenient hour. On this potentially productive day. I can't afford to waste my precious time, but I'm going to anyway. Might as well do it properly if I'm going to do it at all. There have been times where I have gotten home and have thought, Today is the day, but one thing I have learned is that there is never a 'right' day, let alone a right moment. If you wait around for 'that' moment, it's merely a fabrication of a space that isn't really there; an assimilation to fit the schema of perfection.

There is no such schema. There is no such perfection. There is only now.

I'm not a particularly interesting person. I don't have one radical story that will be told for generations. I haven't overcome a massive feat or conquered the unconquerable. I've just been living my life as it comes. However, life hasn't always 'come' as planned, and to those who know me well, I'm a planner. I could schedule every minute of every day if I could. I am definitely the type that would want to be told the future if pseudoscience was in fact factual science.

The reason: I want to be sure that there is purpose. So, I'm making purpose.

And this is why this needs to be written. To let honesty flow—to let go of things I can't always explain. You reading this now means you've been captivated enough to want to know why this is so important to me. The significance lies in the fact that I always knew words would save me. I just didn't know how they would or when they would. I always knew why though, and today the 'why' has been awoken.

July 2020

That first 'download'—March 2011.

I recall that afternoon so succinctly. I was a hot mess.

I was Queen Procrastinator—constantly in fight-flight mode, piloting a plane with absolutely no flying experience or manual. It's kind of cruel but I laugh in hindsight.

I remember that writing felt like the only good thing to come of that day.

Life was feeling strange—a strange that was there to stay for the next five years at least.

The beginning of depression as I playfully titled it: The Mind Monster.

Not fully surfaced yet, but breaking through the ice. One piercing icicle at a time. The diagnosis was really a saving grace in reflection. At least my sadness had a name.

A title.

A cause.

A reason.

Depression without a name was really the most depressing experience I had lived to date.

This too shall pass was the lesson waiting to happen for me, although it would be another eight years or so before the darkness decided to 'pass' for me. There were times when I'd see glimpses of light—the cracks from underneath the doors demonstrating some kind of hope, and then ...

Black.

Thoughts were relentless, unstoppable—racing, to say the least. And the race was never won. Depression has no winners yet there are so many survivors. The statistics show us that the participants in this race are growing steady in number. In Australia, it is currently estimated that one in sixteen people are experiencing significant clinical depression.[1]

This mental process continued through 2011, and the saviour was, more often than not, distraction. Distraction was a beautiful diverter from the truth. It allowed for sad smiles— and sad smiles were better than no smiles at all, I concluded.

In my mind, depression met with its friend, grief, from the moment Dylan closed his eyes and hit a tree. Dylan, a friend to me. The partner in crime of my now husband but then high school boyfriend.

One very cruel and harsh loss to bear for all involved. There is something so very raw and unnatural about not being able to say goodbye. And this isn't about comparing different types of loss—any loss changes your world. But the not saying goodbye.

That kills the soul more than the death does.

That's the medicine in the lesson right there. Because while 'this too shall pass', so does human life.

The fleeting delicacy that it is …

Darkness reframed

Let's begin somewhere in the midst of the union we all know best. The life/death cycle. 'Cycle' for a reason—there is no beginning and there is no end. We depict it time and time again graphically in the form of a circle.

As a race, we know it so well and yet fear it the most. Humans are learning the art of 'change' on a moment-to-moment basis, and yet, do we ever fully learn to accept it? Radical acceptance of what is? And hasn't 2020 been the most brilliant teacher of this concept to date?

What if we took that approach instead and just offered surrender?

There are two fundamental facts that we all know to be universal truths.

1. The presence of breath is evidence for life.
2. The absence of breath is evidence for death.

Innately, we both fear and are curious about death because it's the part of life so unseen ...

As human beings, there is real mystery and fear around the concept of death. In contrast, birth is celebrated and seen as a miracle. It's a culturally ingrained idea that has been embedded for millennia. And, it is the one experience that unites the entire Universe.

Birthing, we all have 'done it'—that is, *have been born*—but the conscious experience only belongs to the mother and the birth partner and those in the delivery space.

There are many people you meet in life who will tell you that they have never experienced 'a close death'. In this sense, it can become hard to define exactly what constitutes the death of someone close because it doesn't have to mean an immediate family member. A close death may also mean that somebody close to you loses a significant other.

The 'second-hand death experience'.

Ultimately, the passing of that soul's ripple effect has a direct influence on how you perceive your own life. Perhaps it is the nature of the mourner's situation being 'close to home' for the receiver of the news that hits hard?

We've all had the dismantling experience when finding out that someone in our community or wider circle has lost someone tragically. You know the type of situation—you bump into someone from school and the chat somehow leads to 'Did you hear about ...'

In its separation, death has the potential to bond people together.

Our current times make these sorts of stories all the more 'real' and accessible, especially with social media often now acting in place of memorials in the form of Facebook condolence pages.

The universal connectedness of the story of someone's passing resonates so deeply because you experience not only empathy for that person you've 'known along the grapevine', but also the instant sense of 'that could have been me'.

It's the universality of death that proves its direct and immediate impact on life.

Before Dylan's passing, I had experienced the 'second-hand death' a few times. Holding space for my own mother who lost her best friend as well as my best friend who lost her mother were profound experiences for a mid-teen to deal with in the space of a year.

I learned quite early on that loss is tragic, hits hard and is often very unfair.

With this also came another hard and fast truth—the Universe never said it was fair. It's running a course so true to Source that it doesn't have time to apologise. Just like the tree doesn't need to be sorry for dropping its leaves during winter, the Universe never said it would promise you beauty in an untouched story.

It's in the raw, messy, screw-up of it all that we find true beauty. The irony in the lessons.

It's in the moments that have us shouting 'It shouldn't have gone that way!' that we learn hard.

There is not and never will be 'another' way.

It almost begs the questions—why do we 'plan' so much in the first place? If Plan B comes to fruition, was it ever really Plan B? Isn't it just 'the Plan'?

Being on this earthly plane, we have no choice but to see things linearly. It's how we are programmed, how we are wired to think. How our calendars ask us to track our months, years, decades.

And so, all along, we are led to believe that we are in full power of our existence. To an extent, we have ultimate power over our *choices*. That's the uniqueness that plays out for us as humans. But do we have control over 'the Plan' …?

Not so sure about that one.

There are karmic forces, past-life trauma, your astrological sign/s, the state of the Universe, and the Collective Consciousness all impacting it … if you choose to allow it to be that way. Or perhaps not?

Perhaps you belong to a paradigm that believes there is no rhyme or reason behind life itself. And that's okay too. But still, even with that lens, the Plan—ultimately how your life is panning out, or isn't—is not fully comprehensible. We are back at square one.

The events of this life are subject to a timeline that we are in no way consciously privy to.

For everything we 'know', there is so much unknown. And universally, there is such beauty in that effortless balance.

Waking to the dark

Let me introduce you to the first time I stared death in the face—literally. I was dressed head to toe in a clinical lab coat. A get-up that I felt I really did have some 'growing into' to do. I remember feeling really detached and agitated because I knew that as soon as our professor unveiled the body, my job was to *dissect* it.

It seemed so misaligned at the time. I had gone about my usual day. Woken up, had breakfast, brushed my teeth, driven with music overloud into the car park for back-to-back lectures all day, had lunch ... and was now to dissect a human body. It just didn't 'fit' in a headspace that was already clinically depressed and grieving ...

So there I was, drowning in my oversized lab coat, and off came the protective sheet to reveal an old man's face—frozen in time, exactly the way he would have appeared when he took his last breath. It felt hideous to then get out a scalpel and 'examine' him. Like the life, the memories he had shared amassed to this—having me, a twenty-something student, inspect his physical body, years on, with absolutely no context to what had landed him on my table in the first place. It felt like I was intruding on his privacy, even though my logical brain was fully aware that at some point, he consented to this.

And that was the first time it really 'dropped'. There has got to be more to this life than what is material.

More meaning than this. The second we ripped off the sheet to reveal the beautiful man's face, it occurred to me how much we in the West are just so comfortable reducing the death experience to the medical model—and seemingly nothing more. If that were the case, then what are we doing it for? Who are we living for?

The student who needed to study the body ahead of her exams?

The idea of a universal balance system really started to land at that point. Firstly, the intersection of the human body and soul. Human anatomy classes are profoundly good at reducing the experience of the body to what we call the fundamentalist or 'medical model' of health. Essentially, the body is compartmentalised. There are specific structures, cells, organs, etc. that interplay with one another. The presence of illness and or disease in the body is the result of one portion of the system breaking down (more on this in Chapter 2). A human body goes about its 'life' until one of these events occurs:

1. Something biologically or chemically goes inherently 'wrong' and starts to unravel the larger physiological systems at play. Eventually, the body has no choice but to surrender to the process and begins to shut down. The cancer process is a clear example of this.
2. An external event outside our control—say, a tragic train wreck—occurs and the classic line of the person 'just being in the wrong place at the wrong time' would be used to describe this type of death experience.

If we are going to reduce the experience of the death cycle at all to fit into one of these two categories, can we try the art of mindful surrender instead? Can we extend the surrender of the body beyond the physical structures that make up human life and try to apply this concept to something bigger than it? Naturally, this begs the question of 'What else?'

What about the soul's process in all of this?

What does a spirit body experience while the human form decides 'time's up'?

Life is fleeting. Blink and you'll miss it. Herein lies the saying that 'this too shall pass'.

Because ultimately, it does. The pleasure, the pain, the jigsaw pieces that make up a 'life' and what it represents—pass, they will. Maybe that's why we are so familiar with saying, 'they passed away'.

What if we looked at every difficult process or circumstance in the same vein?

Knowing that it too will 'pass away' eventually.

Mini death cycles in nature are all around us to remind us that the ultimate let-go is the passing of one's life. The final one at the end.

And yet, we don't have a clue as to when that 'ending' will come knocking for us. We continue to live our lives as though we are entitled to know, though. And then somehow feel cheated if we deem a life cut 'too short' or ended too tragically.

Ultimately, we are human, so we are subjected to our egocentric view of the world. This is not our fault, but it is within our mental capacity to try to understand and work through it.

To cope with grief, we are often well versed as a species to make someone's passing about us and how we feel we have no choice but to pick up the broken pieces of our hearts and continue to live without the loved one for the rest of our lives.

What if we reframed grief? For the purpose of giving our hearts and minds some much-needed relief and solace following one of life's most painful experiences.

It was in my wild and desperate call to the Universe the day that Dylan passed away that the concept of 'grief reframed' landed for me. It really was like hearing news from a comforting voice, although I didn't know where it had come from. It was my own voice, but softly spoken, almost like an internal wisdom source that I didn't know I had at the time.

The voice of intuition spoke of this call to *balance*.

Initially, it was 'the voice' accompanied by a visual. In the visualisation, I saw our galaxy as we know it to be, with the planetary bodies we are all familiar with, but there was a very shaded area around Earth, as if the 'energetic weight' of Earth and its life force was equivalent to the rest of the Universe, as far as we have documented it to be.

As I tried to make sense of this persistent voice, alongside this image, a very simple statement appeared in my consciousness.

> The Universe's job is to balance all the energies coming from Earth, our life force, against the energetics of the Aether and realms you have not yet tapped into. That is why people are 'taken' and often suddenly. Their soul is needed elsewhere. It is beyond human reason but there

will come a time you will understand. The time when your soul is contracted to experience the same.

Well, safe to say, I felt like the definition of a *lunatic*. (I am now, nearly a decade on, really okay with the idea of that label as I find such beauty in following and understanding the role of the lunar cycle; I'm her biggest fan). The voice was so simple but I knew at the core, it didn't 'belong' to me. In that moment, it comforted me and offered me a sense of guidance that I couldn't contextualise. The idea of Dylan needing a fatalistic exit because he was *required* elsewhere was deeply satisfying. Almost like his soul had a 'duty' that could not be carried out on the earthly plane anymore. That in itself spoke to grief in a way that counselling, mourning, and episodes of tears could not.

Intense grief, much like any emotional process, 'shall pass'. It may never leave, but it takes new shape. We coexist with it. Let it not be a thing that we cling on to—to the point of it becoming our identity. Let it move through in waves. We all know that a single wave can never take permanent form. And permanence was never the promise of the Universe.

When the physical body decides it's had enough on Earth, we have the choice to turn that deep and tragic void into something that can aid the healing process. Even space that has seemingly no 'material filler' is the element of air and aether combined, made up of subatomic particles. And so, energetically, there is truth to the notion that there is literally something in existence in the presence of a passing. We breathe in that air. It gives us life. It sustains and carries us through to the next breath and the next ...

Connected, we are.

Infinitely.

Alone, we never could be.

Even if we tried.

Everything else in the grief process is ego doing its magical and uniquely human thing of trying to protect the heart from pain. But even that pain shall pass.

But that is not to take away from the lived experience of loss or to reduce the experience of pain. Loss is hard. Loss is human. And human is hard.

Being human is exactly that —balance in action. Equal parts material and Spirit.

When you've truly loved and lost, you do begin to search for more. The heart and mind, as part of the grief cycle, start the external process of *needing to understand*. The difference is, we can either consciously or unconsciously commence that process.

Death forces us to search for balance in life

It is always an interesting phenomenon to witness someone's grieving experience. The context of the time and place of death, along with the associated cultural backdrop, gives rise to a multitude of pathways of the 'let go' process. There are those who jump straight to logic, spending hours analysing and 'needing to figure out' how the loved one's final moments came to be. This offers solace.

Then, you have those who leap straight to faith, often in a religious capacity. *God needed another angel* is often the sentiment.

The flavour of faith can be spun differently outside the context of religion yet still sit under the safety and guidance of a spiritual umbrella. This is where the notion of the spiritual body departing from the physical body comes into play. The idea that a new relationship with the departed can be sought after. Often, we are grieving the somewhat mundane or small things that contributed to the presence of that human life, like being able to go into their room and borrow their clothes, or the luxury of calling their phone and knowing they'll pick up, or simply sharing a meal together, etc.

The passing itself gives us two choices—

a) Continue to perpetuate grief for the remainder of human life and live solely in memories
b) Consciously embark on a new-found, spirit-guided relationship and deepen our connection with Soul, Self, Other and aether

No right or wrong.

The grieving experience changes based on the conscious choice made. And that choice is the one thing we can control when death catches us off guard.

Those who do not have faith are often grieving the reality of that person's existence in the first place. Many experience their first existential crisis in this space, which begs the thought about life beyond this life even further. The way we dive into our understanding of death and the question of life after someone dies says a lot about where we are at on the journey beyond our physical existence.

The beauty in the quest for balance between life and death

Fundamentally, when we can let go of the *fear* around death, the result is lit-up beauty, appreciation and gratitude. Mind-body-soul practices such as yoga and meditation centre on the art of letting go and observing what comes up as a result, almost in preparation for the ultimate let-go when soul leaves body in this lifetime. The space in between soul and body is where the magic and mystique lie.

If you allow it, the mystery of death gives you permission to remain curious about what is true in your own right. We could even say the inevitability of death challenges you to make the most out of the present on a daily basis. Use the fear of it functionally instead—

Fear of leaving loved ones behind? Love harder.

Fear of letting go of physical self? Nurture your body more.

Fear of letting go of mental and emotional self? Practise more self-love.

Fear of the unknown aether? Escape in awe at the wonder of the Universal system we're in.

Overrun by the threat of death? The more you have to look at and explore.

The bottom line is this—death cannot fail us. It's an invitation for our soul's growth and a call to thrive in our Earth suits. With every day never being guaranteed, you get to choose to accept that invitation on a moment-to-moment basis. The phenomenon of choice is how the Universe expresses balance in every moment. The second a soul leaves Earth and takes flight into the next realm, it creates literal and figurative space for a fresh human being to pass through the birth canal and learn this process all over again.

The lesson

Life and death—the most overt polarity on our human set of scales. The celebration of a newborn baby is no more important or significant than the 'end of life' celebration we've been observing in the form of funerals over the course of time. There is a guiding life-force energy governing our time here with such pristine intelligence it can create the experience of human fear due to the sheer 'bigness' of it all. Approach the dark with as much passion and curiosity as you do the light. Your appreciation for life itself will emerge with more gratitude than you could have ever conceived when you surrender to the most natural cycle of them all.

The same can be said for the experience of depression, anxiety and other major mental health concerns. Depression is akin to experiencing 'mini deaths' of the mind in a continuous loop. It's a mirroring teacher that pushes you towards the light. The soul chooses this mind's channel because it requires a permanent torch to illuminate a path for its own evolution. Depression, as ugly as it can be, is a friend in an unkempt costume. The experience is dark but its recovery is freeing. Recovery is always possible because the peace required to unlock that door was given as a universal birthright the day you took your first breath (let's dive deeper when we end at the beginning in Chapter 9).

You'll come to accept that *this* (whatever your 'this' is) was always going to come to pass because it was necessary for your soul's contract in the grand scheme of existence.

This too shall pass.

Questions for your soul work

1
What are your current perceptions of the life and death cycle?

2
Do you believe that there is more to death than merely the passing of a human body?

3
Are our birth and death dates predetermined?
What influences are driving your answer?

4
How do you appreciate the 'rough' chapters of life?
What resources/tools do you draw on to 'get you through'?

5
What is the role of darkness?
What is your relationship with it?

CHAPTER 2

Homeostasis—Balance in the Body

The Lesson: The Universe is observed at all levels of life. There is a Universally guided intelligence system.

Let's start to pull this whole colossus of a concept together. As I said, *The Balance Theory* is a completely channelled beast. It has a mind of its own and I'm simply tapping into it, to communicate it outward to you. We've started with the life/death cycle to show that balance systems live within and around us, but for the next part of our journey, I invite you to anchor into your body to begin.

Let's ground this strongly—somewhere we can physically witness the magic.

The physical body. It's visceral—literally.

We are about to reduce the enigmatic lessons of Chapter 1 into something more tangible, more observable. We need look no further than ourselves to *embody* the experience of balance in action.

I'll set the intention with you, now, to really feel into the experience of *body* balance. I've drawn a lot of the practical understanding of *The Balance Theory* from some influential yoga classes I've had over the past eight years. And while I can't go past the intrigue of all sorts of upside-down asanas, the most profound yogic practices for me have always seen me surveying the presence of breath.

Matt, one of my most fascinating yoga teachers to date, encourages his students to 'reduce their experience to the breath alone'. This mantra has gone on to be the line that I hang my hat on whenever it 'all seems too much', or I'm on the verge of a panic attack, or I'm losing grip of logical thought. Most recently, this statement was my mental grounding during the pitfalls of a very intense labour and childbirth experience—but that's a book for another day!

Here we go!

Pneuma equals life-force energy equals breath

Breath is by and large the most mysterious physical phenomenon the human body experiences in its lifetime. It is *life force* energy in motion. The absence of it is synonymous with the flashing neon sign reading GAME OVER on the pinball machine.

The absence of breath is physical death.

The documentation of the mystery of breath is as old as our ancient ancestors. The ancient Greeks and Romans were fascinated with a little (albeit huge) concept coined *pneuma*. Folks such as Aristotle, Plato and the Stoics were mystified by the thinking that pneuma aka life-force energy was a gift literally inhaled from God/the Universe/Source and then converted into the physical body. Pneuma was represented in the material form at the seat of the internal organs and their systems. The Stoics believed further that pneuma was a presence that coordinated the cosmos *as well as* the individual body. That is, soul energy was perceived as being the primary catalyst for the harmonisation of the human body.

It was believed that pneuma existed within human beings and in symbiosis with the rest of Universal matter.

Fundamentally, pneuma was considered to be the energetic consciousness that provided function at both a macro and micro level.

Aristotle offered the thinking that the core elements in material form (fire, air, water and earth) coexisted in relationship with pneuma. Amongst yogic teachings, pneuma is aligned with the concept of aether, or the presence of space and stillness that connects us all to higher consciousness.

So why have ancients and mystics been so intrigued by breath?

Because it is the internal compass—the bridge between the spiritual manifestation of our human form and the biology that we inherit inside our DNA at the point of conception.

Breath is our 'ticket in'.

Ironically, breath is the evidence pointing towards life after physical death. It is born from and goes back to the cosmos.

It is the cosmos.

The rapid way that breath shifts in relation to the external environment is the material body's way of showing us that the impulse to self-regulate is Universally guided.

Pneuma is The Balance Theory in observable action among all sentient beings.

Homeostasis—our self-regulation process

In the context of biological science, we call the phenomenon of self-regulation, homeostasis. At the core, homeostasis is a self-regulation process in which the primary goal is to achieve a steady state of function. The perpetuation towards *equilibrium* is the biological goal here. Homeostasis is essentially the governing driver underpinning all of our bio and chemical functions. It is the physical manifestation of the basic human experience if you were to unpack it in raw material form.

By Oxford definition, homeostasis is defined as *the physiological process by which the internal systems of the body (e.g. blood pressure, body temperature, acid-base balance) are maintained at equilibrium, despite variations in the external conditions.* What's interesting here is that the drive towards the homeostatic process occurs *irrespective* of the external environment. The implication is that there is an *inherent physiological intelligence* orchestrating our vital capacity to survive.

Alternative medicine takes this idea a step further with the concept of meridian lines. The theory is that there are acupressure points innately held in the body that communicate in a firing line or channel. Meridian lines link together and impact directly on one another. Practitioners use acupressure to release the meridian and essentially the stagnant energy that has been built up via that channel. Our organ systems and emotions are theorised to coexist in unison based on the meridian in question.

In traditional Chinese medicine (TCM), it is said that an imbalance in the body occurs directly as a result of a blocked channel. *Qi* or life-force energy can only flow in a healthy and beneficial manner when channels are open and clear. The idea is that repressed emotions, if not actively cleared, manifest into physical health problems. That is, the body brings suppressed issues to the surface through its physicality. This helps the person to understand that the area in question needs to be looked at seriously.

For example, the meridian titled Taiyin Lung Channel of Hand involves (as the name suggests) the lung as the primary organ, with the hand being the acupressure point associated with the same. The emotions attached to the lung region include sadness and grief. When a TCM practitioner works on the hand in this meridian line, it 'frees' the channel connected with the lung and the emotions it encompasses.

Homeostatic drives are our innate pull towards freedom.

Balance truly exists in the body when all meridian lines are in check and are clear. If we observe this theory holistically, we can see that this idea is not too foreign from the concept of pneuma. Perhaps ancient cultures have always been onto something bigger than what meets the eye. There are modern-day lessons here.

It kind of goes without saying, whether it be the ancient East or West, the breath/qi/ pneuma/life-force energy/scientific understanding of homeostasis has always been revered as having a level of sanctity celebrated by the human spirit. The 'mindfulness' movement of the past ten years in the developed world has really capitalised on this emerging truth. Never before in our health landscape have there been more apps, podcasts and Netflix specials on the importance of taking time, even if it is just five minutes out of the day, to focus on stillness. The silence of stillness is the greatest tool we have on offer. It's free, it's accessible twenty-four seven and it is a guaranteed ticket into calming the chaos of the mind. We will dive deeper into the phenomena of mental balance in Chapter 3.

Inhale it to embody it

For now, let's look at a simple exercise that can be used to start your day, every day, based on breath work. You don't even need to lift your head off the pillow to participate.

Place your hand over your heart and close your eyes. Observe. Survey your physical body. How does it feel today? Physical awareness begs emotional processing, so feel into that too. Are there emotions tied up to physical sensations today? Just notice that now.

Take a deep inhale to the count of four. Hold in the inhale at the top. Your body will tell you when it needs to release. Exhale the breath to the count of four when your body invites you to do so. Repeat as often and as readily as required. Observe the immediate impact of homeostasis on the physical body. For me, it is often awareness of tension versus relaxation in my muscles that gives me the biggest insight into my state of being.

Use the awareness that arises to 'plan the attack' for the day ahead. I strategise for the day based on the answers whispered in the space between each breath cycle.

Starting the day with this simple task means you've already taken conscious control over the beginning of the day. You've become responsible for your own homeostasis, which is controlled by unconscious centres of the brain—you're already a step ahead before getting out of bed.

Basic breathing in this way opens the opportunity for us to check in with our visceral experience. Instantly, we have access to:

- The pace of our heart rate and ultimately, the state of our own nervous system.
- The health of our digestion (especially considering the gut-brain connection. More on this below).
- The extent of tension/relaxation in our muscles and joints (i.e. a direct ticket towards understanding our stress levels).

All three of these elements (when acutely brought to our awareness) can be consciously 'corrected' and utilised to our benefit.

Let's explore further.

Our heart rate operates in direct relationship with our central nervous and respiratory systems. Our brain stem, the very raw and primal part of our brain, has complete reign over the heart rate. It's an unconscious process. This is the reason you are still considered 'alive' when in a declared coma state. In this state, the brain stem has continued doing its thing while the cortical brain matter, aka the 'thinking brain' (the part that has developed as our species has matured), is dead. The heart rate continues to beat on, independent of our conscious awareness.

The heart rate is our fastest tracker, keeping tabs on whether our nervous system is in a state of stress. You may have heard of the 'three Fs' or the 'fight, flight, freeze' response. Essentially, our nervous system is in constant dialogue with this unconscious mechanism that basically governs how we are going to manage the response to a stress-based stimulus. Of the three Fs, one response pattern is usually dominant over the other—we either fight the threat, attempt to escape the threat, or freeze (i.e. a full-body startle reaction).

In opposition, a steady and 'happy' heart rate informs us that cognitively, we are experiencing a state of *calm*. 'Sittin' on the Dock of the Bay' style. This aspect of nervous system function is affectionately known as 'rest and digest'. As the term suggests, a content nervous system is directly related to happy 'pipes' and comfortable plumbing—that is, healthy digestion. There is a reason that 'number twos' happen to come out easier when we are at home or in a regular routine—the nervous system isn't competing with the stress we all experience when needing to poop in public!

Given that the heart rate and nervous system go hand in hand, an increase of nervous tension equates to an elevation of the heart-rate. Most people can recognise this state of being as anxiety. With one in five people experiencing this state at clinical levels (i.e. requiring formal intervention or some sort of therapy), there is no surprise that as a society we can almost say that at least twenty per cent of individuals are experiencing dysregulation on a cellular level. If we blow this out and observe it, a fifth of us are fumbling along as nervous wrecks to some extent or another, going about daily life.

It kind of begs the question: Surely the shitshow we are witnessing every day on socials, the news and any other mass content portal can be attributed, at a grassroots level, to this collective loss of homeostasis on the biopsychosocial plane?

Our cells—our physical bodies deserve better.

We are the mirrors mimicking Universal calamity

Okay, so back to the larger context downloads I received about the interplay of cellular homeostasis and its place in *The Balance Theory*. Energetic exchange is occurring in constant motion. It has been this way since the beginning of time as we know it on this 3D plane. Since our human bodies are 'mini universes' in their own right, what happens to our physical body is a minute, albeit crucial process that contributes to the balancing out of material energy in the greater aether. As individuals, we contribute to the wider homeostatic landscape of all earthly beings. Think of it like this: we are each a key player in the spiritual ecosystem. That is, the homeostasis that exists between Earth and the realms beyond. We participate simply by having an Earth suit.

A little esoteric, I know, but when I sat with it, this idea really helped me to accept how vastly different people's experiences of health and wellness can be. It permitted me to radically accept the myriad of *dis*ease states that a single human body can experience in its lifetime. It offered an answer as to why so many people who have touched my life have died too young from the hideousness that is cancer. It spoke to why I've had to treat patients who have suffered from significant stroke under the age of ten who were otherwise 'healthy'. It gave me the understanding that while we have free will, there is a large aspect of Universal intelligence that we simply do not have control over.

To surrender to this notion is not to lose our power or forfeit the right to make choices.

The surrender of control in the context of health and illness is our power. It is a true acceptance of the state of our Universal calamity. It accepts that as mini universes, our bodies are simply reflecting the chaos of the aether. It is a natural by-product of universal homeostasis.

When your body experiences health and vitality, it is a reason to celebrate and to practise gratitude at the highest level. When your health somewhat betrays you or your body systems fail, it's a chance to get curious and lean in to what else may be experiencing imbalance in the wider context of your life.

Our bodies are merely mirrors mimicking Universal calamity. We are designed for imperfection.

Be kind to yourself.

Of course, 2020 lessons appear here

2020 was an incredibly strange year globally, as I'm sure we can all agree. When there is imbalance occurring collectively on a mass scale, such as a full-blown pandemic, you can almost guarantee that on an individual plane, some kind of chaos would be bubbling away under the surface. I found that throughout the year, almost everybody I interacted with—and especially in my close circle—was experiencing some kind of personal turmoil. The kind that brings you to your knees and completely unravels you in order to build you back up again. My version of this was a little more subtle with its lessons (cheers, 2020).

Fast forward to Easter weekend, April 2020. I found out, thanks to an intuitive nudge, that I was pregnant.

From the get-go, I decided that I would surrender control of the pregnancy. I'd attempt to do it with the healthiest non-attachment possible so as to escape any kind of disappointment that may arise.

Easier said than done.

Around me, there were several beautiful friends and family members experiencing miscarriage and infertility issues, so in order to protect my heart, I decided to 'let go, let God' with the idea that my physical body was only half the story seeing the pregnancy into fruition.

Ten weeks into what felt like a relatively cruisy pregnancy (I escaped the dreaded 'morning sickness period'), I received a phone call from my obstetrician.

'Natasha, I'm sorry to inform you that you have gestational diabetes.'

My gut reacted in a way that I didn't see coming because, well, as you will recall, I had decided that I'd surrender control and practise non-attachment.

Safe to say, I was attached to this diagnosis.

Immediately, a hundred thoughts flooded my mind.

But I eat really well. I've always minded my sugar intake.

I know a million people who would be more susceptible to this—they eat like crap every day.

But I meditate and exercise.

But I do 'all the things' and take all the right supplements ...

INSERT SPIRAL OF ANXIOUS THOUGHTS HERE.

And yet, the reality set in that the hormonal systems growing my placenta —which was growing my human were faulty. How awkward for me to accept.

I was relieved to learn that Bub was not going to be majorly impacted by this. Instead, it was me who was going to have to learn a whole new lifestyle, diet and eating regime *on top* of a very stressful time at work, *on top* of a pandemic.

How inconvenient.

And while to this day, I still hold the highest gratitude for the health of my baby through that time, there was a piece of me that really felt that my newly reinvented pregnant body had failed *me*.

Why?

So that I could fully appreciate the value of homeostasis?

So I could embody the importance of physical imbalances impacting mental imbalances? (More on this next chapter.)

At the end of it all, I could not control the onset of gestational diabetes. It had nothing to do with my health pre-baby and everything to do with the placenta that was forming to nourish my tiny, albeit needy little babe.

Our human bodies are fundamentally imperfect—as is

everything else living in this 3D world. And as intricately designed as it is, it even gets its own homeostatic drives 'incorrect' at times when variables are even slightly manipulated. Hormones are the biggest culprits in this space.

Our bodies are the manifestation of imperfection in cellular form. This is a universal truth.

The offset of nourishing the beautiful little being inside me was insulin resistance requiring medical intervention. All the energy vibrating through my vessel was solely focused on ensuring the safety of my child. With this reframe of mind, I was able to radically accept that the disease state of diabetes was in fact necessary to secure the health of my bub-to-be.

This realisation absolutely fascinated me. I had no choice but to recognise in real time that, human body to human body, we are seeking equilibrium. This is an evolutionary goal for our species.

After all, the body has a lot of work to do to ensure homeostatic balance. We quite often do not stop and take a moment to send our body systems thanks and love.

When science meets spirit, it lands in the body

There has been a long-standing belief across many societies over time that our human bodies or 'Earth suits' are in constant communication with the soul that inhabits the body's material form. This exists over the course of our lifetime. We are starting to mass subscribe to the idea that the Universe has had this plan for our bodies all along. Self-enquiry has never been more tantalising, especially in health and wellness communities. Anecdotally, I've definitely observed a rise in the everyday person wanting to find out their birth time to go to town on the analysis of their sun, moon and rising signs. I've found myself increasingly surprised that this vernacular is becoming more mainstream.

For me (as a closet woo-woo), growing up, astrology gave me a raw understanding of my energetic makeup. My Gemini Sun has me communicating these words to you now. The channelling for *The Balance Theory* has come courtesy of my Pisces Moon—all that governs my deeply spiritual and intuitive emotional self. The Capricorn Rising in me has allowed me to sort my shit and nail this whole glorious mess of ideas into one neat and coherent read for you all. Regardless of the self-enquiry framework you subscribe to or entertain, science and spirit like to speak to the same concepts in different costumes.

Universal balance must be achieved first amongst physical homeostasis in an individual body, it then takes form on another level when each material being balances out amongst the energetics of the aether.

Enter musings on the body's relationship with the chakra system. Let's dive into an analysis of where the physical body transcends and shares energy with the entities beyond the material SELF.

The chakra system is our radar for physical imbalances when we are tapped into them

If this chapter were a tertiary course, your prerequisite knowledge would be an understanding of the chakra system—i.e. our energy centres and their role bridging our physical, mental and spiritual bodies. Here's crash course 101 just in case this is your first time landing on this concept. The idea here is that a chakra imbalance directly impacts a physical body imbalance because of the intrinsic relationship between physical body and energetic body. The presence of disease is arguably reflected in the chakra imbalance. The physical manifestation of the disease state is how the Universe is communicating with us. It highlights when we need to check our homeostatic state and then reattempts to balance our body systems in order to achieve the evolutionary goal of 'health', aka survival of the fittest.

Chakra, the Sanskrit word for wheel, refers to the energy centres that are housed within certain physical points of our material body. The subtle point where spirit meets body is home to energetic touchpoints that represent core aspects of our lives here on the 3D plane.

There are seven core chakras running physically along the spinal column. When we dive into the study of human embryology, it's absolutely fascinating to note that the first core structure of our human form begins as a spinal column. From this column, our vital landmark structures—heart and head—then manifest. Our energetic bodies are essentially formed in unison with our vital organs. Science and spirit are definitely hand in hand throughout human gestation if this example is anything to bounce off.

The root chakra

Imagine you're sitting spine-erect in a seated position with legs crossed—the lotus pose, if we consider meditation. Starting at the base of the spine, we find the *root chakra*. Energetically the colour red, the root chakra gives rise to all things material possession and survival based. Think financial foundations, basic experiences of health and the foundations of 'home'. Corresponding to this energy centre is the area of the lower back. Any sensation in the lower back can be completely debilitating if we've managed to hurt it in any way. A lower-back issue can result in us being unable to complete basic activities such as walking and physical exercise. The result is a snowball effect on other areas of wellbeing. This can then impact our capacity to work, earn a living, or contribute to society in a basic material exchange. Our root is the crux of our spiritual and material experience. Without it, the foundational and more nuanced aspects of our lives are often limited.

The sacral chakra

Up from the root chakra lives the sacral. Mapped on the body, the sacral chakra resides at the level of the navel. If you were to cut deep into the organ systems, it is no coincidence that a woman's uterus finds home in this exact position. The energy of the sacral chakra is revealed at this precise location—the centre of all human creative potential.

The ability to form life anew.

To practise creativity is to tap into our birthright.

It is the most sacred art we can perform.

Anything that requires innovation mixed with flow state is creative. We are all creative. If you can breathe, you can create. It's your God-given dance with the rest of Universal matter.

Blockages in this chakra can often look like a 'rut', whether it be creative or sexual in nature. Unblocking this region is essential for experiencing the sensation of effortlessness and pleasure—a state we are wired to want to achieve, in order to thrive.

The solar plexus chakra

At the level of the gut, we welcome the solar plexus. I intuit the solar plexus as being equivalent to a hug from an older sibling. This is the house of internal authority. The home of your intuition.

Your true sense of self.

By *Self*, we mean the mirror reflection of your ego but also the soul part of you that holds your highest alignment. It's no wonder we often say intuition is a 'gut feeling'. It is precisely that—a visceral gut pull towards your sense of truth.

Biologically, serotonin—our 'happy' neurotransmitter—is partially produced in the gut. Yet again, another circumstance where we are observing our birthright pull towards happiness and flow state—the energy of our gut, the seat of our intuition, is synonymous with the energetic centre responsible for our authenticity.

If we look at microbiology, the latest research in the space of the gut microbiome suggests that an imbalance of gut bacteria has a direct impact on healthy brain function, and essentially, homeostasis. It makes sense that the gut microbiome decided to sit in the space of the solar plexus when the genetic lottery was considered. When something is simply 'off' in the gut, your intuition is attempting to inform you, through your body, to check your authenticity in any given moment. A gut health issue can be so overwhelming that your mind is forced to consider it— if you go against your intuition, then the body has a sure-fire way of making sure you attend to it. Physically, this may come through as the sensation of 'butterflies in the stomach' or cramping, bloating and other funky bowel-related issues. As unpleasant as this might seem, the solar plexus in its expression of the gut microbiome is really your greatest ally and most obvious internal compass.

The heart chakra

Heading north of the solar plexus, we land smack bang in the middle of the chest. The heart chakra. The midpoint—the official crossover between the lower and more 'earthly' chakras and the upper and more 'spirit centred' chakras. The heart chakra is located in the same physical region of our heart and lungs. Our vital organs show us how crucial balancing the heart chakra is. The centre of pneuma is housed here. An 'open heart' in this situation means to energetically invite the healthiest attitude towards living.

Essentially, the ability to accept, surrender and let go as often as required over the course of your lifespan resides in the heart chakra. Living with a balanced heart chakra looks a lot like radical acceptance of your emotions and emotional processes. When aligned, the heart chakra is emotional safety and trust amongst Self and other human beings. It is the ultimate space holder.

When the inhabitant can fully embody the loving energy of the heart chakra without limit or condition, the next chakra, the throat chakra, can operate freely.

The throat chakra

The throat chakra is directly linked with self-expression. It is an open channel for free speech, hence its physical location. It is thought amongst homeopathic communities that the throat and sacral chakra communicate in order to coordinate forms of self-expression, marrying the gap between who you feel you are and who you *say* you are. Creativity, residing in the sacral space, is most beneficial when it's freely communicated.

A block in the throat chakra also means blocks with sexuality, money and self-worth. A suppressed throat chakra often finds its answers 'down below', so to speak. Further to this, the heart chakra needs to be open in order to communicate from a place of love, compassion and understanding. Safe to say, it's pivotal in cultivating healthy relationships and freedom of self-expression.

The third-eye chakra

In between your physical brows, you'll find the 'third eye'. Metaphorically, this energy centre houses your intuitive insights, the capacity to tap into your inherent 'knowing', and the bridge between your physical body and the spirit beyond the earthly form. A clear third eye sees a person having a strong sense of intuition and the ability to act on that without hesitation and with full-body confidence. When cleared, it also facilitates healthy reasoning, future planning and the potential to dissolve ego. It is often said that mental health issues are evidence for a blocked third eye as the mind is quite literally clouded by distraction and delusion.

When you think 'third eye', think the practice of meditation. The act of meditation is the surest way to flush the third eye and keep it working to your benefit. Meditation on the third eye is also said to connect to you the greater collective consciousness. Psychic input also lives in this energy centre for those tapped in.

Suffice to say, you want an opened third eye if you truly wish to participate in your reality.

The crown chakra

The crown chakra—our final and arguably most potent chakra.

This chakra lives above the crown (your head) and connects you to the infinite Universal space. The energy in this centre is said to transcend the realms of time and space—allowing our current version of Self to connect with past, present and future variations of our soul. It *is* our spiritual guidance when we are tapped into our true alignment. Think of the six other chakras as the important pieces of the Jenga tower. If we are a brick loose, we can't possibly tap into this higher level of Self. Spiritual practices create palpable methods for us to experience the phenomenon of the crown and embody the same.

When you're owning your crown, you really are sitting on the throne and overseeing your entire existence from a place of pure peace.

An open crown elevates the human experience.

When it's healthy, your physical homeostasis is the natural by-product.

The chakra system is an in-built homeostatic barometer. The science of it resides in organ systems. The system itself is a perfectly curated dialogue between the body and the emotional, mental and spiritual elements of Self. It serves as an intricate reflection tool. When you breathe pneuma into your energetic centres, you are consciously creating homeostasis. You are the living example of what we are all attempting to touch.

Balance.

First in the body, in order to achieve it in the mind—and

beyond.

Let's play with this idea further in Chapter 3 when we dive deeper into balance processes of the mind.

The lesson

Pneuma is life-force energy pervading our physical bodies and the space around us.

It is the critical factor indicative of life.

Breath is our touchpoint. The one thing that ensures we keep going in this Earth suit.

The Universal goal for balance is at work at every level. Our cells require it for function. Our emotional body demands it for wellbeing. Our organs thrive when systems are balanced. Our chakra system is the meeting of science and spirit landing in our bodies. It is our in-built guidance system and can be used as a practical 'check in' tool to examine our state of homeostasis.

Health, wellbeing and balance are one inherently integrated system.

Questions for your soul work

1

Are you conscious of pneuma in your own body?
How often are you consciously breathing?

2

What's your relationship with the homeostatic forces in your body? Are there any signs coming through from breath, heart rate, or digestion that suggest subtle imbalances? How can you attempt to rebalance these processes through acts of self-care? For example, going for a run or a swim is a quick and sure-fire way to regulate your breathing. Commit to one rebalancing action today. If you're unsure how to do this, enlist the help of the myriad of wellness professionals out there!

3

How is your physical and emotional body feeling right now as an entire unit? Drop into a moment of presence and check yourself via the chakra system. Work your way up from the base of the spine to the crown. Scan for imbalances in a moment of stillness or silent meditation. Jot down whatever has come up for you. Awareness is key to self-regulation.

CHAPTER 3

Balance of 'the Mind'

The Lesson: The mind is the gateway.

The relentless art of seeking mental balance

The stream of consciousness that spoke to me the night that Dylan passed away was recognised first and foremost in the place we all spend the majority of our time. It's a place that we literally recognise every single moment of waking life and somehow we don't spend much time 'decorating' it to be a space of utter enjoyment and delight—for the most part.

Welcome to your own unique 'place'.

Your mind.

What a field.

The Balance Theory's lessons and landings have come through my mind's eye—the third eye, energetically speaking. You'll recall from our chakra learnings that this energy centre is the space of visualisations and realisations. But it is also a place where delusion and misguided thinking can leave you totally lost if you have limited navigation skills in this area.

In the world of science, the space that thought occupies lives in neural structures supposedly responsible for executive functioning and higher-order planning. Conscious thinking is a process that I have come to learn has very little to do with your overall capacity for wellbeing. Cognitively though, we seem to believe that what our thoughts offer us are the 'be all and end all' of our value as a human. We spend most of our cognitive energy 'up in our heads' and whether we are aware of it or not, it now takes deliberate effort to ground into our bodies.

On the Earth plane, the mind does not register the world around it without the body to filter it through. We've forgotten how to receive our bodies. This is the crux of imbalance when it comes to mental health. We judge the thoughts that are *judging* us. This is where mental health can start to unravel if we don't have a mental first-aid kit to help ourselves.

After ten long years tending to my own space, fluffing the pillows and doing a major renovation, I can now confidently say to you, my reader, that my mind is an inviting space that you'd probably wanna come and hang out in. Like eighty per cent of the time. The other twenty per cent is reserved for my shadow self. This space enjoys a striking decor, not quite Gothic, but quite cold and often clinical.

Marble, pristine.

Bone-clinic white.

It's sophisticated but it's nothing like the ambience of your grandmother's house.

But it is beautiful. Because it is the epitome of light meeting the dark. Light exists because of the principles of shade and shadow. It is a symbiotic relationship.

Universally, we weren't promised a conscious mind full of rainbows and unicorns. And yet it's quite simple. We are led to believe that if our rainbow is more of a pre-lightning-storm gloom or our unicorn more resembles an old, over-the-hill donkey, then most likely, we're mentally broken.

You are not broken.

You have likely fallen victim to the mental prison of unconscious thinking like most of the Western world. It's not your fault. While we were in school learning to recite facts and figures without any critical questioning outside of that realm, we weren't taught how to harness the racing monstrosity of the mind.

Learning to tame the monstrosity is what can literally save lives.

It is no wonder that this world is experiencing a collective self-worth crisis. We've forgotten that our mind is seeking balance. Darkness and uninvited thinking are merely a part of the path to equilibrium.

Mental homeostasis—it's an art form.

During the final year of my undergraduate degree, I was determined to expose some truths about the lived experience of mental illness among Australian university students. I devised this project because, at the time, I was part of the thirty-percent statistic[2] and wanted desperately to reduce it. Published in 2016, our team's findings concluded a few key points that continue to be relevant today:

a. Diagnostic labelling of mental health conditions can cause confusion, which contributes to mental health stigma across the board.

b. All forms of media—in particular, social media—can be both productive and counterproductive to the portrayal of mental health and illness. Young people are susceptible to mixed messages about the state of mental wellbeing because media is consumed in unprecedented amounts across multiple platforms. That in itself is overwhelming.

c. Psycho-education programs should be implemented at a younger age to help prevent the onset of mental health conditions in early adulthood.

While our study focused on a small population size in the context of our global landscape, the takeaway message here is that now especially, with post-pandemic levels of isolation to contend with, our mental health crisis deserves attention.

Our search for mental wellbeing is mentally draining. Mental imbalances are arguably responsible for other areas of life (i.e. our financial situation, relationships, environment and career) being so off kilter.

Let's force that beast into balance, because it is important for human survival.

In recent times, once I had fully come to process the fact that my mind was equal parts anxious and creative, loving and kind, the ultimate gift was handed to me: I had scratched the surface of mental peace. I had surrendered. After living most of my youth with a lens of clinical depression and severe anxiety, my mind came to show me something different.

My mental struggles were my creative power.

I had finally *embodied* my mind.

I'll start this section by saying, no, I am not a clinical psychologist. In this space, however, I am a long-term consumer of mental health services, as well as a life coach. Mindset coaching challenges our thinking and behaviour in order to bring about actionable change and real shifts in perspective. Much of what I'm about to share is a combination of my experiences. From consuming the system, to counselling my clients in my role as a speech pathologist, to the lessons I've learned as a health science researcher, and of course, through life coaching my beautiful client community—both in a one-on-one and group capacity—I have found there is much to be said about the art of seeking mental balance.

You are not your thoughts

If there was something I could gift to you, the reader, right now, it would be the soundest piece of truth that I have ever received. It may have been said by my psychologist, it could have been a product of my obsessive reading on the matter, or perhaps I first heard of it during a yoga retreat. I can't be sure. But what I do know is that this one piece of truth can literally change your life.

You are not your thoughts.

Perhaps this is the first time you've experienced the above statement, and—like me the first time I goggled at the thought of me not being my *thoughts*—you may be a little confused or disbelieving.

Let me explain.

The process of thinking is a mental faculty. It makes us human.

Truly human. Like the ability to speak, thinking sets us apart from our other mammalian friends. It is our blessing and our curse.

Blessing—we can use the commodity of thought to shape the way we want to live.

Curse—we can use the commodity of thought to sabotage and get in the way of how we want to live.

It's our very own, personal double-edged sword and yet nobody ever teaches you to *think wisely*.

The most beautiful and cruellest part of human existence is the fact that we are subject to thinking. In Buddhist teachings, thoughts are the basis of all suffering. Essentially, being subject to thinking *is* the experience of suffering.

I'm sure you can recall a time where you've had a thought and then thought: *Where the hell did that come from?*

The lived experience of mental illness is perhaps the greatest torture you could ever endure. It's silent and it can be deadly but it is also super powerful. With the right help, you may even come to find that your illness is your superpower.

It took me ten years to actually embody that and make it my reality.

Two months ago, I engaged in a final[3] therapy session with my beautiful therapist, Mandy. She was quick to remind me of my very first session with her, back in 2011—the thick of depression and a fresh wave of grief on hand.

'Remember when I told you that "your monster" is actually the very thing that has given you the greatest blessings in your life?'

I smirked at Mandy through the camera. (Our sessions had gone to telehealth during the pandemic.)

'Yes ... I remember.' I laughed with her and at the memory of my former self. For that brief second, I held space for the version of me that had first headed to Mandy's office. Anxious, strung out, depleted and carrying a deep sense of loneliness. She seems long gone now but I continue to nurture her through times of stress and intense mental flare-ups. They're rare now, but they still happen.

I'll paint a very sad picture for you. By sad, I mean helpless. There I was, a twenty-year-old woman: endless possibilities lay before me and I was riddled with fear to the point of it paralysing my entire decision-making process. It hijacked my executive functioning to a state of constant confusion and mistrust.

We won't linger in this space for too long, but it is completely critical to the understanding of The Balance Theory playing out in the mind.

There was nothing more jarring than the experience of knowing fully that the one thing that had gotten me 'so far' in my young life was the very thing that completely debilitated me that year.

In 2011, I lived in the shackles of an unstable mental state. Anxiety created many a catastrophic thought in my mind and made 'living in my head' like attending a film in a cinema with the doors locked. Even if I wanted to look away or disengage from the visual, I still had the auditory content on repeat.

Booming and inescapable. Torturous at times.

Most of the time, the auditory loop was full of harsh and profane language, textured by voices that often didn't belong to *me*. It was quick to remind me of every insecurity and sense of low self-worth that had ever penetrated me, too. In that moment though, my mind was an imposter, leading me to believe that I owned every horrific voice that filtered through my stream of consciousness.

Not fun.

In my peak state of unwellness, I remember having the visual of attempting to remove my literal head and place it on my bedside table at the end of the day. It was some kind of whacked attempt to remind myself that, given the choice and the means to the end, I would have literally severed myself from my mind to have some shot of mental space.

And that's where I, like many of us, was completely misguided.

The truth is, you'll never be able to sever your head and get rid of your mind. You are left with only one choice. You must learn to coexist with it. Insecurity, mistrust, fear and all. These states of mind are just that—states. They are impermanent. They will pass and can change at any moment. The key is to learn how to 'state change' so that your mind works for and not against you.

You are the nemesis and the hero in your own mental story.

Overthinking, overthinking

I was prescribed antidepressants—a popular brand—off the back of one trip to my GP's office. There wasn't much to it except the instruction to wait out the two-week period. Over that period, they were supposed to 'kick in'—and not without the knowledge that mentally, I was 'bound to get worse before I got better'.

Well that sounded like crap. The idea that to get better, I had to get worse first. It didn't make sense.

I wanted to hit unsubscribe on that email chain, thanks.

After feeling more confused leaving the surgery than when I had entered it, I went to the local chemist and begrudgingly filled the script. There they were—thirty pretty little pills in my hot little hands, all promising me one shot at happiness.

I drove home, then stumbled through the door to gather my books for my next lecture before heading off to class that day. I popped the blister on my packet of promises, dispensed the pill … and threw it in the bin.

That moment to date is one of those memories that I'll never forget. I decided then and there that if my mental illness started in my mind, it would end right where it started.[4]

That day, as deflated and let down by Self as I felt, I learned that there was a piece of resilience that was *always* accessible to me regardless of my mental state. I worked out, years down the track, that that day, I was tapping into my intuition. This was the part of me that knew inner peace was available to me, but I was too disillusioned at the time to fully recognise that for what it truly was. With a strong meditation practice and daily journalling, I worked out my flow in terms of getting a hold over my mind.

My intuition was confirmed during my first therapy session. Mandy explained to me in a very 'CBT'[5] manner that our thoughts are almost the last thing we are processing although they are the first line in the stream of consciousness that we are tapping into.

'If we acted on every single flipping thought that went through our minds, this world would be a thousand times more messed up than it already is ...' Mandy nodded along with herself as she explained further, 'So how can you be your thoughts entirely?'

I had no words to say but a lot of disjointed questions running through my mind.

She had a point.

I was intrigued and fed up with myself at the same time.

Fed up with thinking.

I ended up attending regular sessions with Mandy for the next eight years. With her incredible guidance, I learned the art of non-attachment to thinking.

The brain versus the mind

There is a very real distinction between the brain and the mind. This distinction can save lives.

Mandy helped me to unpack the above statement during some preventative therapy sessions I had just before giving birth to my son. Due to my history of clinical depression and anxiety, I had booked in a few sessions to see her before my induction date. I was determined to get on top of my predisposition to postnatal depression before it even had a chance to rear its ugly head.

My official diagnosis is primarily obsessional OCD. Basically, it means my brain has some faulty neurology that can sometimes catastrophise even the most basic of situations. The OCD loop in my brain can be extremely dark and worrisome. OCD-type thinking is the act of converting every thought into its 'worst-case scenario' without your permission. It happens on autopilot, without consent. It's the intruder who broke off their ankle bracelet. The alarm is silent. It's uninvited and yet can set up camp at the most inconvenient of times. It also loves to attack the things you love more than anything in the world and stamps all over beauty.

The anxiety component of the illness is that part of you that fears your thinking will never be normal again. It's illogical, but its experience can be so real it causes panic attacks that have an emotional resonance for days, sometimes weeks.

I was almost expecting OCD to flare up postpartum, purely because my OCD loved to feed off anything unfamiliar and thrived in unprecedented territory. Throw a newborn, sleep deprivation, and lack of time and usual resources in the mix and I had a breeding ground for some pending chaos.

In full-fledged proactive mode, I sat face to face with Mandy, preparing to gain a whole new world of strategies as I got ready for my whole new world.

She started: 'What if the mind lived beyond the brain? Our latest research in the world of OCD is really starting to show that this could be plausible. In the case of OCD, we are now starting to think of it more as a neurological glitch, rather than a psychological problem—that is, your brain's feedback loops might be 'faulty' in terms of its hardware, but your mind and its software are NOT the cause of your condition.'

I liked this idea immediately. It gave me more reason to isolate my sense of true self, my inner peace and calm from the illness. In this model, the OCD truly wasn't *mine*, but an *experience* running through faulty hardware. In this instance, the brain—the cells and all its neurology—was dishing up some unfiltered content that wasn't in the interest of wellbeing. That's it: nothing more, nothing less.

So I say to you, reader, if we entertain this idea for a moment, then wouldn't that mean that the mind that runs your world doesn't necessarily belong to you?

What if your unique mind was on loan to you—what if you are currently *borrowing it* from the rest of the Universal calamity?

How freeing is that thought?

If thoughts are borrowed and downloaded by some faulty neural hardware, aka your brain matter, then that's merely a portion of your human makeup. In no way is it your *whole* get-up. In no way is your mind *you*.

A part of, not the whole of.

Therefore, a mental illness can be seen as part of you, but it is definitely *not* you. There is so much more beneath the surface than meets the eye.

Parts put together help us to balance, whereas a 'whole' is finite.

You can't balance material that is finite, but you can balance *parts*. Therefore, could it be that by material nature, the brain is able to experience clarity, true balance? Your brain is segmented in parts. If you dissected it, you'd physically be able to label and recognise them.

But the mind ... the software we are all storing away in files ... you can't physically identify its home.

The mind must then be responsible for unifying the parts on its search for balance. The mind helps the parts run like a well-oiled machine. A mind tuned into a healthy vibration is the manifested experience of peace. Our journey towards this state is the universal quest for balance in action.

In that moment, it made total sense. If we are on this perpetual quest without a manual for mental balance, then our mental capacities must be parts of the system but not the system itself.

The Bottom Line: The mind is both within you and outside you, but *not* you—just like an illness is a fragment of a whole, but not the whole itself. You can stand back and observe it. By no means is it your identity. *The mind you're privy to/tapped into, in the realm of thoughts, is your own personal conversation with Universal calamity, but that conversation is as borrowed as a library book.* You can choose to return it, or borrow something new at any time.

Part of experiencing fluctuating states of mental health

is likened to changing the channel. You're in control of the remote. Be impeccable with your energy, flip the script (i.e. the stream of thoughts running through your head) and choose the content you want to consume.

We will explore conscious reframing of the mind below.

The true power of the mind is the ability to choose something different when it benefits you and to communicate your choice with the rest of the world.

I live with OCD and have done so for as long as I can remember. Obsessive-compulsive disorder is a condition of my physical brain but I *choose* something different when it comes to my mind and the channel the illness hosts.

OCD in my mind's eye is now as such—Oh! (O) See (C) divine (D). My illness gave me the entry ticket towards understanding my divinity; faith in the life beyond this life. The collective consciousness that is bigger than my human condition and any 'fault' that comes with that continues to be OCD's biggest gift to me. My gratitude practice is derived from my direct experience of OCD. I found that I consciously started to document my appreciation for the simple things when I felt my mind was experiencing peak calm. A day without obsessive thinking really was, and still is, pure bliss.

Joyous existence.

Em*body*ing the mind

I was coaching a young client of mine a few years ago when the lesson I'm about to share sunk in deep for me. Billy, a sixteen-year-old boy, had a lived experience of chronic pain. He was also emotionally intelligent enough with his own body to recognise that much of the pain was a product of how anxious he was when he woke in the morning before school. In sessions, he was able to rate the pain on a scale of one to ten (ten being the worst pain of his life) and over time started to correlate the eight-to-nine category with the expectations around exam periods or the social requirement to participate in a school function.

In the end, it was a combination of deep psychological work and conscious hypnosis, coupled with breathing techniques, that pulled Billy out of his head and into the pain. He eventually learned the art of surrender to the experience. In the yogic world, he became the observer and dropped the 'active participant' role of the pain. He was beginning to use his mind to speak to his mind-body intelligence.

One late Thursday evening, on my last appointment for the day, Billy entered my room, looking defeated. It had been two weeks since he attended school because his pain sensation meant he couldn't get his head off the pillow in the morning.

'What's going on, Billy? I haven't seen you this flat in a while,' I started carefully. He often took five minutes to open up. Today was different; he spoke with a conviction I hadn't heard in his voice before.

'I just feel like, it doesn't matter how much work I do on my mind, I always seem to fall back to this feeling of underlying anxiety. It's like the voices can't ever really be silenced.'

I smiled and thanked him for his honesty.

'Billy, I don't think the goal for any of us is to really silence those thoughts.'

He looked puzzled, and as he often did; he loved to challenge me.

'Well then, why am I here with you? What's the point in all this?'

I closed my eyes for a brief minute to collect my thoughts. I pulled on all my resources, and was filing through my mental toolkit when the clearest metaphor landed for me.

'Billy, did your mum take out the garbage this morning?'

He looked at me like I had three heads and gave a half smile.

'Tash, where is this going?'

To be honest, I wasn't sure, but I kept speaking, trusting what was falling from my mouth.

'Imagine what it would smell like if Mum didn't take out the garbage today.'

'Mhmm.'

'What would it smell like?'

'Just a tonne of … crap, really.'

'Correct. So I'd imagine that you probably wouldn't want to hang out in the kitchen if the garbage was rotting away there, right?'

'Right …'

He stared at me intently and slightly puzzled as I went on.

'Imagine our brains are filled with mini containers that can only hold so much rubbish. Over the course of our lifetime, we fill these containers with waste that often comes in the form of emotional baggage, unpleasant memories and, in some cases, trauma. There are specific containers for positive stuff too;

it's just that it can be hard to find these containers amongst the mess. From my experience, we are really good at finding storage for the containers holding the crap, we just aren't well equipped to *empty* them.'

I watched as Billy mused over this idea. His curiosity piqued.

'I don't think I've ever emptied out one of my containers—and there are plenty up there!'

I smiled at just how swiftly he had hooked onto the metaphor.

'Billy, we have so many containers that are full to the brim and we continuously buy more to hold more. Except, that's the thing; our brains can only hold so much information. Eventually, the stuff inside begins to rot. Especially when we haven't been taught how to empty the containers and refill them with helpful and beneficial items.'

'This makes total sense,' he replied.

'Back to my original tangent; imagine Mum had a kitchen full of containers of food and had run out of fridge space. She'd have bags of rubbish piling up in the kitchen in no time. I don't think anyone would want to step foot in the kitchen after a week, let alone a year, or a lifetime!'

Billy nodded along, fiercely.

You get the picture.

Our mental health deserves a cleansing—on a regular basis. As often as you'd throw out the daily rubbish bin. After years unkempt, the material wastes away—and definitely not in a sustainable compost-like situation.

Globally, our state of mental health is more like landfill.

Hard, cold plastic thoughts. Fabricated in factories that are so distant from our truths and with no sustainable means of rectifying the reality.

But there is another way, just like there is renewable energy. You carry it on your person, because *it is* your person. It's your vessel. Your body is your material radar detector. When you are 'in your body' or in your flow state, you have direct information about the current state of mind that you're tuning into.

Using your body to manipulate facets of your mind equals the balance we are seeking.

We can go one further by exploring the idea that your health is dependent on your body's ability to receive and churn through emotions, fluctuations in mind states and the cellular process of our biology. Piggybacking on this idea from Chapter 2, retention of our emotions literally plays out in your body.

Think of the process of anger. You feel the clench of your muscles, your jaw braces for battle, a pit of rage accumulates in the gut region. The release of the muscles and the subsequent visceral response has to go somewhere. If not exercised through physical practice, the emotional process filters back through your cells and pockets itself, literally in your muscular walls, in the form of muscle tension. Energetically and emotionally, you receive this message in the form of reactivity; that is, long-term frustration in the mind.

Every day, make it your basic health mission to get into your body. Find the thing that gives you your unique sense of flow. For some it's yoga, for others it's the ritual of slowing down to explore the sensory experience of coffee drinking. Maybe it's putting your face in the sun for five minutes on the back step.

Our heads are overrun and are begging for our bodies to step up as the nurturer.

Conscious versus unconscious processing

How do we fine-tune the frequency of the mind? It seems like such a mammoth task. And it is. But arguably, the thing we need to do most to get there requires the least amount of thinking. It's simple, really.

There is a multitude of things out there that you'd read about. Many a 'do this' and 'don't do that', but fundamentally, there is a reason our bodies offer us routine periods of unconsciousness. And there is an art to it.

Sleep.

Put your head on a pillow with the intention to rest.

That's it. Most of the time.

We are in a global shortage of it. We live in times that idealise the hustle and place one of our most crucial biological needs on the back foot. We look down on it. Almost like our worth is tied up in how many hours we didn't get last night. Sleep deprivation is a slow and silent killer. At the very least, it is killing off our precious neural circuits and weakening the ones that have been planted on shaking ground by an already wound-up nervous system.

If we cast back to the chakra system, we could place sleep at a 'top and tail' position. It lives in the root chakra as it speaks to our basic needs. Essentially, if we don't have adequate cognitive rest, over time, we die. Running to the other end of the spectrum, how can we possibly connect to a higher purpose if the precious architecture that oversees all basic functions—the brain—doesn't have time to tap out and recuperate?

Our third eye is praying for some shut-eye too.

Suppose we accept the idea that the mind imprints not only in the cells of the intelligent system that is the body, but also resides in the emotional and cognitive centres of the brain. Logically then, it would make sense that the field that the mind resides in requires rest and restoration too? This is the biological function of sleep.

As a new mama to a beautiful baby boy, never before had there been a time that I, like the squillions of mothers before me, so needed to devour every last drop of sleep. Literally: wherever I would get some shut-eye in those days, I'd take it. Ridiculous, but I had even fallen asleep on the breast pump. Not even my nipple getting stimulated, churned and yanked could keep me awake during the early motherhood daze.

This is not an uncommon story; it's simply evidence that the body and mind will switch to 'do not disturb' when it has no steam left in the tank.

Fresh from the sleep-deprivation postpartum camp, I can confidently say that the frequency of the mind—that is, the content that is displayed to your mind's eye—has a tendency to fluctuate depending on the time that you're paying attention to it. My 3:00 am mind has a very whacked and irreverent channel that it tunes into compared to my sensible and practical 8:00 am brain. We've all been there: that text message you wanted to send while your mind spiralled with infinite possibilities as the clock clicked over to 3:47 am seems ludicrous as the sun rises. There is a reason that the word lunatic is associated with crazy—the moon mind is free spirited and limitless, while your sun mind literally sheds light on your action plan.

Both are valid and equal. Both are creative, brilliant and functional. It's just about learning to use each state to its full advantage. Think of it as though the sun mind is there to *hold* you, while the moon mind is there to *expose* you. The sun mind is your conscious processing and the moon mind shows you your shadow—the stuff you need to work on and move through.

Ebbs and flows

Our minds are omnipresent. The mind is a stream of consciousness that lives within a field that Source allows us to 'tap into' on a needs basis. Therefore, we can perceive our unique mind **as a gateway** towards experiencing a higher form of conscious intelligence; essentially, the link between our material reality and our emotional/spiritual reality is realised in the space of the mind. The function of the mind is how we *make sense* of this intersection of human experience.

Our minds exist within us, for us. They are the direct channel that we tune into to *understand* and *process* our human experience. There are schools of thought in philosophical and esoteric texts that suggest our minds are also interacting in a force field that surrounds us. This is the argument for the idea of a collective consciousness. The notion here is that the frequency within our own mind directly plays alongside and intermingles with the vibrational frequency around it to equate to or 'call in' the physical reality. That is, we can't ignore that aiming for mental balance to experience states of joy and peace involves the process of balancing out the energetics of the physical and vibrational space around us. There is merit in this thinking, which will come to light and make much tangible sense as we explore concepts of higher consciousness in later chapters.

Basically, physics allows us to measure vibrational frequency, so we have evidence that the field around us physically exists. The question is what takes up the energetic space *within* the vibrational field—what is its purpose? We could argue that that space in the field is the collective consciousness—the channel linking us to Source/the Universe/God/The Thing Bigger Than Life Itself.

Our minds are conditioned. They are susceptible to change based on that concept of nature and nurture. Nature in the sense that our minds run intelligently through the canals of the nervous system in our bodies. Our minds can manifest their expression in the physical realm and in a mental capacity. By physical manifestation, we mean the signs and symptoms that present in our physical health. You can perceive signs and symptoms as the clues that give us the 'heads up' regarding our current state of being.

By mental manifestation, we're talking about the experience of thoughts and consciousness. What we think, feel and believe contributes to the quality of the lived experience.

The makeup of our experience is subject to the conditioning

it has received through upbringing, childhood experience, culture, race, religion, sexual orientation, technological advances and societal expectations—basically the external world around us that interacts with our state of being. It's almost impossible to list all the components that are impacting our minds, but just the acknowledgement of the magnitude of influence is enough to make you realise just how susceptible we all are to mental fragility.

Early in 2018, I had a significant flare-up of my OCD. In fine form, it loved to sneak up on me during major life transitions. At the time, I was six months into a very healthy marriage, but OCD does not discriminate. If anything, my form of it attacks the most precious pieces of my world. I had also just started a very stressful medical speech-pathology role and so the anxious mind was off and running.

This time was different. Fresh off the back of studying mindset coaching, I invited this flare-up with curiosity. Curiosity and coaching go hand in hand. Encouraging an air of curiosity is half the process towards making major life changes. The person in focus is asked to question and speculate about the root of the current situation in order to get to the bottom of it and make lasting change.

I coached myself through this one. Through my clinical work, I was definitely not a stranger to a toddler in meltdown. Having worked closely with autism spectrum disorder throughout my career to date, I was also very *comfortable* with the idea that, at times, it is not unusual to experience sensory overwhelm. This often happens when our internal processing does not align with the external environment.

I got super curious about this.

While I was not a toddler melting down over the taste profile of my dinner, I was an adult melting down over significant change to my life circumstance. There is not much of a difference between the two. The toddler in this situation would have been thrown by the lack of control they had coming into their dinnertime routine. Me, in my full adult mind and makeup, was thrown by the change in routine: the day-to-day being unfamiliar and unpredictable.

I was craving control at an all-time high.

So I surrendered to that and threw it all away. Accepting the fact that I was out of control was the best thing I could do to grab a handle over the situation.

At a conference on sensory processing only a year before, I learned that we have two key opportunities to set ourselves up for a successful day. If we miss these windows, it is not as though we are going to have a failure of a day, but we would have to act more *effortfully* to turn events around in our favour.[6]

These windows are:
1. The final half-hour before bed
2. The first half-hour upon waking

In terms of brainwaves, we are functioning in a hypnotic/meditative state during said periods. That is, gateway access to the unconscious mind is wide open, or at least as wide as the unconscious mind will permit. It is often said that approximately ninety per cent of our decisions and actions are subject to the functioning of the unconscious mind—the part of us that often doesn't even get a look in. As children, we operate from this state until about the age of seven. That's why, for so many experiencing ongoing trauma and psychological challenges in adult life, we need look no further than early childhood for the clues surrounding why such patterns have continued into our adult lives.

Dancing with the fresh bout of anxiety I was experiencing, I offered myself to myself as tribute and consciously carved out a ninety-day experiment to see if I could make any dramatic shifts by using these windows of opportunity.

It looked like this: for ninety days, I would journal in the last half-hour (or thereabouts) prior to sleep and first thing upon waking in the morning. This specific form of journalling had four key goals:

1. To consciously 'release' any form of stress or anxiety from the day so that I wasn't taking unresolved stress to bed
2. To tap into insight that my body was offering me for 'clues' on my mental/emotional state (as discussed in Chapter 2)
3. To gain conscious awareness over the emotional state I was bringing to bed/taking forth into my day
4. To set a gratitude intention for the day

I would then meditate as a ritual to cement the realisations that I actualised during the journalling process.

To say there were profound shifts is an understatement.

By day ninety, I was waking up, radiating energy, and feeling extremely eager to start my day—no matter what was on the agenda. Depression and anxiety took their rightful back seat in the corner of my mind and the general cognitive fuzziness that was floating over my thinking (or 'cog fog' as I affectionately named it) had completely dissipated.

I was gobsmacked, but not overly surprised when I thought about it. What I was doing has been neurologically proven to restructure our neural wiring. I was literally taking my neurons and manipulating them to work in my favour during windows of conscious hypnosis that occur naturally in between waking and sleeping. In the world of science, we call this phenomenon neuroplasticity. It is a breath of fresh air in the space of neuropsychological research and it is *powerful,* to say the least.

Besides the obvious increase in gratitude for the small things and pronounced mental clarity, I was also cultivating a sense of kick-ass confidence, purely because I had total awareness of what emotional processing I was taking into the day. I was then able to choose actions and make decisions around this.

For example, if I woke up fatigued on a Monday due to events over the weekend, I made sure to factor in a 'down time' activity on my lunchbreak and an evening meditation sit to clear the cog fog before bed. If there was an uncomfortable work conversation to be had with a colleague or client, I was energetically prepared for it and actually felt fortified when speaking—regardless of the outcome.

My dreams were also more *useful* during this time. Intuitive downloads were heightened, and unnerving, anxiety-driven themes lessened by the second month. It was incredible to witness.

Awareness is our friend. It gives you the means to foster day-to-day balance. Awareness doesn't care about the happenings of our day-to-day lives. It just gives you full autonomy so that you can show up for your life.

To be self-aware is miraculous weaponry.

Another bizarre observation came out of those journal recordings. Because I was noting down every waking thought upon rising in the morning, at times, I would wake with a song stuck in my head, or a movie line on repeat, or something auditorily obscure. We've all been here before. What was really interesting was that there was a pattern with these recordings. A song that I was obsessed with on Monday would be front and centre in my musings upon a Thursday morning wake-up. A jingle I heard on Tuesday was the first thing on my mind on Friday.

Seventy-two hours seemed to be the unconscious processing timeframe for these seemingly medial thoughts. I decided to apply the same concept to my emotional processing by day thirty into my experiment.

Yes, again, another thought-provoking realisation.

The events of Monday seemed to be emotionally *realised* in my unconsciousness by Thursday morning. For example, if I had had an argument with my husband late Monday evening, I'd wake up with frustrated feelings towards him, for seemingly no apparent reason, by Thursday. Sometimes the emotional processing occurred as conscious thoughts approximately ten minutes after waking, and other times, I'd have a dream about the situation on Monday during my REM sleep[7] in my Thursday morning slumber.

This pattern was real and it was a total mind blow. By day ninety, I was almost able to predict feelings, emotions, thoughts (and even which song would be stuck in my head) three days ahead of them eventuating.

I was manifesting my conscious experience.

This experiment is available to us all, for free.

The lesson

This chapter is not a manual on manifestation, how to meditate for overall wellbeing, or how to facilitate gratitude. I encourage you, dear reader, to practice all of the above; because combined, these rituals are a recipe for abundant health.

But I will say this.

Invest in your conscious awareness over at least ninety days.

The mind truly is your gateway to physically creating control over your world. Balance is a natural by-product of that level of awareness.

To take back our power is to recognise that most of our decision making and belief systems are controlled by the unconscious mind—the parts of Self that we don't have direct access to without specifically altering our brain chemistry. Meditation and mindfulness tasks manipulate our neurology, which in turn impacts the frequency at which our bodies are receiving the messages from the field around us. I would argue that both meditation and mindfulness practices are essential for healthy living in a post-pandemic world.

Seeking balance in the mind is to realise that we are working with both the internal and external environments that contribute to our current state of being. Radical acceptance that our minds are impressionable (and often take on 'negative' impressions as default) allows us to surrender our thoughts and experience states of peace and joy beyond the thinking modality. It's almost as though, to really dive into serenity, even if for a moment, we have to endure the human faculty of thought as a trade-off. While the ratio of thought to peace seems scarce and somewhat 'unfair' in terms of time spent in either state, the result in the exchange is *still* the experience of balance.

Bliss outweighs anxiety any day.

Even if fleeting.

Even if momentary.

That's your gateway to spiritual health and wellbeing. You have an in-built power in the form of neuroplasticity to consciously change your wiring and manipulate your mind to work for and not against you.

That in itself is material balance, ready to play with the world around it.

Questions for your soul work

1
How does the idea of 'the brain not being the mind' sit with you? Have you observed this in your own life?

2
What is your current relationship with your mind in its many facets?

3
What does mental health mean to you?

4
What are your self-care practices around mental health?

5
Do you perceive your mind as the bridge between your physical and emotional/spiritual health? If yes, in what ways does this occur for you?

CHAPTER 4

How We 'Human'

The Lesson: Authenticity is the universal motivator.

The need to belong—eleven hugs a day to feel connection

I once read somewhere that as human beings, we need approximately eleven hugs a day to meet our emotional needs. Eleven. Apparently, the oxytocin release (the 'love' hormone that is essential to the feeling of connectedness in life) that comes from eleven hugs helps us to chemically achieve emotional homeostasis.

This hug prescription is a biologically driven need.

With gratitude, I am fortunate to say that my quota is met with a newborn baby under my roof these days, but it really got me thinking about people beyond my household. I don't know that I could confidently say everyone receives up to eleven cuddles a day. Do people even know how to practise self-love and care on a daily basis to achieve their emotional balance needs? It seems like a pressing thing to start a conversation about. We all deserve to have our basic oxytocin release for the day. Especially because, in theory, it is not that difficult to achieve, and yet with today's Western lifestyle, we have reason to believe that it might be.

This also rings true when we are looking at our global

mental-health pandemic. Earthlings, as 'back of the hippy van in the seventies' as it is, we really need to learn on a mass scale how to hug ourselves so that we can hold the others around us.

Let's begin the deep dive into the realm of energetics and emotional balance. Neurologically, we are wired—physically and chemically—to have a purpose-driven team around us. A baby without a village would die without the nurturers of their pack. An adolescent without their 'people' becomes ostracised and delinquent. An adult without connection becomes detached, void and wry to the point of apathy.

We are at the pivot point on our journey, where we start to observe the notion of balance in action, beyond our individual selves. From here on out, *The Balance Theory* will explore the role of 'us' as individual units on the same team and the consequence of this role in the context of that which is outside of ourselves. What is our place in creating either balance or imbalance within our relationships? How does this concept ebb and flow depending on the nature of the relationship dynamic? Does an energetic union between two complete persons impact the energy when it comes to a wider web of people? How does this affect a community, a nation ... the whole human population?

If the Universe's goal is to experience itself—chaos and all, calamity and calm—then it just makes sense that innately, human relationships are a reflection of that exact mirror. They are bound by universal laws that (often) get a little hectic!

Energetics of relationships
—be impeccable with your energy

A few weeks ago, sitting around my parents' island bench with a cup of tea in hand, my youngest sister, Jo, and brother-in-law, Sam, were engaged in a tiresome chat. It was 10:00 pm on a Thursday night and Friday was looming, but aside from that, they looked particularly burnt out. I was picking up Alfie, my son, after a long day, but I realised that there was a discussion to be had before I packed him into the car to start the night-time 'baby go to bed' routine.

'What's up?' I said, concerned for the both of them.

'Tash, you know a thing or two about the laws of energy or something like that. How do you protect yours when you are forced to do things or see people out of obligation?' Sam's voice was more tired than his face at this point.

A few thoughts flooded my mind at that moment and they are important to share here with you all.

Firstly, we are not *forced* to do anything. We only feel this way when we are operating so far from our values and truth that we start *reacting* instead of consciously *acting*. Secondly, when we engage with others due to sheer obligation—whether it be family commitments, networking engagements, or catch-ups that are based on 'I should' rather than 'I want to'—the only result is total energetic depletion; total imbalance.

Detachment from a situation, person or cause essentially creates tension and feelings of disharmony in the mind and body. In the realm of social psychology, this concept is called 'cognitive dissonance' and it is exactly that—the result of one's beliefs, attitudes and values misaligning with one's actions, behaviours and current version of reality.

Having grown up in a large ethnic family where your second cousins are treated as close as your siblings, my siblings and I are no stranger to feeling the need to meet the expectations of others. I truly believe that I chose this beautiful albeit exhausting family dynamic because I had some hard learnings to experience around energetic boundaries and protecting my own energy in this lifetime.

Ignoring your need for boundaries, especially in an energetic space, sets you up for a strong and *reactive* form of cognitive dissonance. The thing with this form of dissonance is that it lives heavily in the mind and manifests emotionally with feelings of frustration, resentment and shame. As we've learned from Chapters 2 and 3, these emotional states need to be flushed through the system somewhere and so we usually direct that energy into one of two channels:

1. Our own bodies, to the detriment of our physical health
2. Others, which in turn creates disharmony in relationships

Neither option is ideal and for good reason. Humans are intrinsically driven towards their authenticity. When we aren't in energetic alignment with what we intuitively know to be our truth, the result is the mind and body moving into a space of disconnect. The disconnect itself is our compass. It is the message that signals deep to the core that we must pivot towards what we are *really* seeking. If that pivot feels jerky, rigid or as though it's *just. not. happening*—then that really is your biggest Universal sign.

Cognitive and subsequent emotional dissonance is your blaring alarm bell. It warns you that the 'thing' in your pathway is either not for you in the long run, or it is a lesson that is *required* for you to be able to energetically hold the next thing that is likely a more authentic version of your truth.

This is not a new idea. Many a 'wellness guru' before me has discussed this concept, but I want to assure you that energetic alignment is one realm where intuition is somewhat 'proven' by the wonderful world of science. The sheer psychosocial presence of cognitive dissonance theory in action shows us first hand that humans really are driven towards outcomes and behaviours that create comfort and pleasure.

It's instinctual.

It's unconscious.

It's intuitive.

It's our actualised quest for harmony.

It's our fascination with balance in full form.

In this circumstance, Sam was hitting breaking point with the number of social engagements on his plate. He felt a massive aversion to attending the family function on the weekend but couldn't quite put his finger on why. The answer was ragingly obvious to the wallflower in the situation. Sam's energetic need (i.e. to rest and restore) was compromised, and we could aggressively say that his personal boundary was violated.

Boundaries that are set (or not set) in the context of human relationships are an exploration of the universal laws of attraction. What resonates at the same frequency—or 'wavelength', as Sam would say—moves toward each other. Human cells literally do the same thing; they are inherently programmed to move in the direction of where they *need* to be. Scientifically, we call this process osmosis.

Osmosis is the unconscious force in human cell biology by which the molecules of a solvent transfer through a semipermeable membrane (that is, a living cell) towards a solution of concentrated solute value in an attempt to equalise the solute levels on either side of the membrane. Jargon aside, this is another perfect example of our body's desire to experience homeostasis.

Humans are learning to play energetic osmosis with one another. Sometimes, we are not very good at it—and most of the time, it is an unconscious process. We are often simply floating about our lives, with no firm boundary line and no respect for who or what energy we are allowing to cross through our membrane walls, so to speak. The mental faculty of cognitive dissonance is the radar detector within the experience of our energetic lines becoming tangled—pay attention to the clues.

Our discussion that night led me to the words 'Be impeccable with your energy.' It felt finite and definite as the words hung off my lips. In that moment with Sam, I decided that I too needed to practise what I preached a little more. Once I had made that decision, almost overnight, I vowed that any action moving forward would have to be driven by my innate value system only. It needed to feel impeccable, recharging, authentic and aligned in order for me to participate in any activity or pending invitation. When we live with this level of integrity, of confidence, we are saying to the Universe that we know the worth of our energy and we deserve to be interacting with the people, environment and circumstances that are going to offer betterment to our being. When you know your worth and you action it accordingly, you'll sing your own praises in the form of gratitude for your life and what you already have. It's a delicious space to be in.

The example of Sam in this chapter opens up a voluminous discussion regarding the result of our boundaries being crossed in the long run. Because we can't set up an electric fence to ward off unwanted vibration, we need to get really good at using our minds to form a mental one.

This is an ideal time to introduce you to one of my best friends, Mitch. Mitch and I are two peas in an energetic pod. You'll come to know his story a little later on, but for the purpose of this segment, Mitch and I were noticing a particular pattern amongst our close family and friends at the time I was writing this chapter. Over the space of a week, we had both encountered a multitude of stories with the same theme. Amidst our circles, the theme of toxic ancestral lines was running deep. So many stories around inner-child work, parental wounds and lineage healing were circulating. The person in question would be spilling their truth and realisations of the need to clear a toxic relationship, and/or answering the call to reconcile with a parent or core family member, and/or seeking advice on how to set up a practical method of knowing where one's energy starts and finishes.

The 'how do we do this' was the key question on everyone's lips.

The perspex box
—I'll hold myself so I can hold you

Both Mitch and I have a long history of being empaths. We are that category of human that apparently radiates the 'dump your sh*t here' sign. I used to wear this sign as a badge of honour.

These days, after *a lot* of practice, I choose to cultivate more of a 'feel free to occupy this space with total love and respect but you will also leave when I politely request you to do so' kind of vibe. Years of clinical practice and a lifetime of personal development has led me to master the art of being able to hold space without taking the baggage of the other person on. In saying that, it's a work in progress.

Intuitively, I feel called to share my top energetic secret with you, my reader, the same way that I explained it to Mitch that particular week. I want you to walk away the most present version of yourself when it comes to entering the arena of holding emotional space for others.

Here it is: Place yourself in a perspex box. When you find yourself in a situation with a person who is zapping rather than adding to your energy, envision a glass box around you. The box is glass so that you can see the person clearly. They can feel your love and support, however, the glass barrier serves as a protection for you—to see and not to 'take on'. If the person enters the space of victimhood or is projecting their stagnant or worrisome energy onto you, it simply fogs up the glass, rather than penetrating your energy.

The perspex box is honestly the single most useful and accessible mental tool that I reach for. The best part about it is that it does not impact your capacity to truly be there for someone. It just means that you are ensuring that the oxygen mask is actually fuelling you first. It also signifies to me, personally, the very real reminder that I am not responsible for the feelings of others and similarly, I am not responsible for one's emotional process. There is a multitude of factors that shape an individual's reaction to a stimulus (that's another book for another day!), so it's helpful to remember that we are definitely not the sole cause for any reaction that presents. We are, however, responsible for our reaction to that process, person, emotion. Ownership in this sense makes for a good-quality human. When I'm working clinically, this tool is one hundred per cent available to me at any given moment. It allows me to move on with my day and to keep my energetic body (or *aura* for those in the spiritual space) intact.

Being aware of your energetic integrity is taking this concept and aligning it with your physical, mental and emotional health to set yourself up for maximum gain. The result of the gain? The ultimate version of who you show up as; authenticity is the universal motivator. I am yet to meet someone who doesn't desire or demand meaning and fulfillment out of their life (remember, a misaligned action is fundamentally the behavioural form of cognitive dissonance). If we explore the essence of depressive illnesses, the illness itself exists as an absence of the core ingredient of our *being* as humans—that is, a longing for deeper connection and unity with Self.

Energy Expired

'Energy is either constructive or destructive, Natasha! We know this, because a very famous man many moons ago suggested that it can't be destroyed, either. It's just a matter of where it's channelled!'

She practically screamed at me down the phone. An odd sentence to be hearing on the end of a client call, right?

But God did her message land loud and clear.

I was having a phone consultation with a very dear client of mine. Let's call her Katie. Katie is a loyal and loving mother, but at the time we were having this conversation, Katie was tired. Tired of fighting for her kids' right to access services in a system that couldn't cater for them. Katie was also tired of advocating for her children with special needs.

The context of our conversation that day was this: Katie had just finished making a formal complaint to a government department about how her children's emotional needs were not being met despite having the supposed 'protocol' in place to do so from a schooling perspective.

She would often tell me that she was smacking her head against a brick wall in order to get some action moving in the right direction.

Katie's comment that day was blurted out of sheer frustration. But she was totally right. Energy is energy. It cannot, by physical or spiritual property, be dismantled, nor can it come undone. It can only be transmuted.

To an extent, we have an element of control over its shapeshifting ability. We can choose to be impeccable with it, when it is projected onto us. We decide if it's constructive or destructive. When I channelled what this idea meant for *The Balance Theory*, the insight I received was two simple yet resonant words: *Energy Expired.*

This download came through with exceptional clarity.

We are often asked, on an intuitive level, to drop the armour and decide when our effort in controlling the energy flow of a person or situation is valuable or not.

Energy Expired is a theme that we will continue to discuss as we run through the next few chapters. At its root, the concept is this: While energy itself cannot 'expire' (it can only transmute), our relationship to that energetic line can. The idea here is that we have the power to decide what stays and what 'fizzles' when it is no longer serving us. If we take the reins and choose to step away from an energetic boundary for the betterment of ourselves, then we are choosing to detach from that energetic line. In the spirit space, this is likened to the 'cutting of the (energetic) cords', except this idea revealed itself to suggest that Energy Expired is not a permanent player in the game: we also have the power to decide when energy is reactivated for our personal benefit.

This will make much more sense when we discuss the energetic properties of relationships in Chapter 6 and when we first come to realise our Travelling Partners—the true players in our personal game. Energy Expired is a crucial piece about energy being called, somewhat needed, elsewhere. Think of it in the context of 'something's gotta give'. When you let something go, quite literally, you're opening up space for new lessons and opportunities to fall into place. You single-handedly create the material and energetic environment for that manifestation to be held.

The thought behind 'expired' implies that, for you, that thing/person/place/circumstance has completed its full-circle lesson for this moment in time. Either you energetically don't require it or them for your higher purpose moving forward, or that energy—the weight of said manifestation—is *Universally demanded elsewhere*. The implication is that no matter how hard the pill is to swallow, surrender is for the Universal best.

Even when it makes no sense.

Even when it wasn't 'planned'.

Even when it 'wasn't supposed to go this way'.

Even when you truly *thought* you knew your endgame.

Ultimately, you don't.

This is the part where the Universe steps in and works the masterful plan in collaboration with you.

Energy Expired is accepting the part you've played in your material world actualising and then officially handing the baton over to the overarching life plan.

Universe redirects—transmutes, if you will—the energy

where it needs to be. Universe knows where energetic service is required. Universe knows how to play the balance game because Universe created the rules. We are merely the pawns in the grand scheme of it all. Universe is the literal game changer.

Universal language

Universe is a simple communicator. Universe speaks purity—the language of innocence.

Universe speaks directly to Child.

The inner one that lives inside your heart space.

If you want direct answers about Universe's plan, speak to your inner child. The part of you that is ever-present as yourself, the child, before the rest of the world *conditioned you*.

They know. They've always known. They are liberated and unconditioned. They know the reason you decided to play life (perhaps again).

Everything you need to learn/express/heal is held in the hand of your inner child.

We are so quick to disregard the childhood version of Self because it behaves *like a child*. It's raw, unfiltered, and often lives in imagination. You notice that those three words are also used to describe Universe.

Raw.

Unfiltered.

Imagined?

From the next chapter on, we begin to go outside of ourselves to follow the Universal crumbs.

The lesson

Energetically, *how we human* is a deep begging.

A yearning to be seen. To have our fellow peoples truly see beyond our masks. Love us. Hold us. Know us. Be with us.

The part of us that inherently screams, *Meet me where I'm at and love me anyway!*

Love me anyway.

Unconditionally—regardless of circumstance or life condition.

The motivator behind this lifelong mission is *authenticity*.

This expression of authenticity is the version of yourself as the inner child. The inner child is the purest and rawest version of yourself. The rest of 'you' grew around that persona and was subject to the distortion and dissonance; the blueprint Universal chaos that exists in and around you. You co-created the inner child in deep consultation with Universe.

To find balance with our current self, we must truly get to know the inner child. It is from that place that we can springboard and interact with Other and the rest of the world surrounding us.

The child demands that their boundaries are intact in order to have their basic needs met. You are the adult, the parent for that child. You set the boundaries and you are also autonomous in ensuring that they don't get crossed without your consent. You automate when energy expires and when it reactivates. This piece is critical in the arena of wellbeing.

A free inner child brings a sense of peace to Self.

When Self is aligned, we open up to play with the rest of Universal magic.

Questions for your soul work

1
Do you have a conscious relationship with your energetic body? Are you aware of your personal boundaries and how to keep them in check?

2
What are your current practices in keeping personal boundaries? Are they serving you?

3
What does living an aligned life mean to you? Are you in that space now or does something need to change?

4
What's your current connection to the idea of Universe?

5
What are the 'crumbs' of your inner child teaching you right now?

CHAPTER 5

The Divine Dance

The Lesson: Balanced bipolarities create space for truth.

The Principal of Balance: A manifesto

Life is ceremonious.

We live in an environment of bipolarities. It is a universal law. Everything in and around you is made up of two ends of the same spectrum.

This is The Divine Dance.
This is balance in action.

We are all trying to touch the sacred pause.

The Pause is our pulse.
Our safety.

The reminder of our primordial state.

Understanding and appreciating the bipolarities of earthly life is the true essence of consciousness recognising consciousness.

Mother Earth shows us the beauty in this perfect mystery when dawn cracks open and we witness the awe we feel in the presence of sunrise. The fleeting point in time where there are equal shades of dark and light.

We are governed by the magic in the middle. The momentary space where, just for a second, everything is perfect.

Everything is balanced.

We are reminded of our divinity when we take the time to truly absorb the observation.

I breathed out this download with very strong clarity. It spoke with conviction. Nature does not make a single processing error and neither did the writing of this piece.

You, my reader, are invited to participate in The Divine Dance. The exploration of life's opposite ends of the spectrum. The observable truth that Universe finds purity in spacious 'in-betweens'.

Collectively, we're all attuned to the sentiment of 'everything in moderation'. Nature takes this sentiment and presents it in the form of material creation. Nature has Universal intelligence backing it, allowing for ease of state transfer. The flower can only bloom by basking in exquisite temporal conditions. Equal parts ebb and flow, of rest and movement.

Of stillness and static.

If we walk through life with two left feet, we experience disassociation. We're denying the flow in the dance. Mentally, we are dissonant.

As we have previously explored together up until this point, we need look no further than our physical bodies and the operation of mind and emotion to observe the inherent desire of Universe to experience itself through us.

The common driver is the pull towards equilibrium.

The harmony arises from this relentless pull towards the centre.

Fluidity, by way of definition here, is the exact point of the spilling over—the tipping point, if you will—that shows that neither this nor that is one hundred per cent our truth.

Black and white exist so that shade, the grey, can be seen.

Validated.

All versions are uniquely gorgeous.

All variants of the grey.

Grey creates rainbows.

All flecks of shade.

And this is the thing that has time and time again been missed.

Collectively absent is this realisation—

Human beings are by nature, grey.

The material world is black and white.

Our consciousness takes elements of the black and merges them with the white to find home in the in-between.

Nature seeks joy in expressing grey.

An amassed amount of darkness swings the pendulum too

far and throws out balance. Similarly, the presence of constant light means we can't appreciate it. In order to appreciate the presence of anything, we need its bipolarity to *actualise* that recognition.

One exists, because the other does.

The birth of the in-between—

Is grey.

Nature's Cycles:
An introduction to masculine and feminine energy

I'm sure, in the age of social media and sharing that we are all in, you've come across a post or two about fruit being shaped like the organ that it supposedly serves. Take, for example, the walnut looking like a tiny brain, loaded with all the fatty proteiny goodness to keep your thinker thinking. Or the cross-section of a carrot, which not only looks like an eye but helps us to see, coming stocked with all the vitamin A that your retina requires. And beyond fruit, my personal favourite is the dendrite pattern of a tree branch looking almost identical to a human lung—the source of our oxygen exchange.

A few weeks ago, the avocado imitating a pregnant womb refreshed on my Instagram feed. Likely because of all my baby-related following, but nonetheless a beautiful reminder that made me smile. Apparently, the avocado takes nine months to ripen. The 'pregnant' phase for the avocado blossoms much like a developing fetus—the avocado waits for the perfect timing to be birthed into the world (and plated up as the most delicious smashed avo you've ever consumed).

Just like the concept of art imitating life, natural life cycles like to create art of their own. If you are really looking, you'll find that nature leaves clues so subtly and in the form of synchronicities to assure you that everything is literally divinely planted.

That's the way Mama Nature chooses to comfort you.

The cycles spell safety.

Nature's cycles live symbiotically with us to prove our innate divinity.

We need to pay undivided attention if we want to tap into this in-built natural security system.

Up until my pregnancy, I'd always had a tumultuous relationship with my moon cycle. For readers not attuned to this language, a 'moon cycle' is the hippy-dippy name given to the menstrual cycle. And named after *la luna* for good reason. The cycle itself, just like lunation (the cycling through of moon phases), is approximately twenty-eight days long. It has been long documented in sacred text that the moon cycle is directly representative of one's emotional journey. In religion, the moon is often a repeated motif suggesting that God is present as 'light' during both the day and night. In the tradition of tarot readings, the depiction of water represents the unconscious processes at play due to the moon's reign over the tides.

Search most texts and you'll find that the moon has been worshipped as a goddess in her own right for centuries, likely beyond human documentation. Fascinatingly, in cultures both East and West, the moon is the one subject that both parties bring to the table with sheer respect and idolisation.

The inherent difference, however, is that in the West, we attempted to conquer the Moon by literally placing humanity's boots all over her surface (the act itself says it all). Throwing it over to the East, we see the moon was the universal embodiment of the woman herself.

Soft, luminous, ever-glowing and instinctively mysterious.

The ripening and retreating nature of the moon as she moves through her cycle from new to full mimics, almost exactly, the ovum as she moves from the ovary to the womb, ready to meet her fate. In peak ovulation, the ovum shines so scintillatingly, much like the full moon. Women's wisdom tells us that the moon is most attractive in her fullness because she is willing to display her most honest form, the truth of her beauty. Her undeniable authenticity. Ovulation proves the same, as a full and healthy ovum literally translates to fertility. The actualisation of new life. The cornerstone of the human life cycle.

The authenticity of woman in her uniqueness—the potential to hold pregnancy and carry out the birthing process—is life force in action.

Really, it is beautiful.

Nature provided us with an art form that you simply can't destroy because the process is so intricate and pure, it demands reverence.

The role of the masculine is to provide the other side of the equation until the product is nurtured enough by the feminine compeer and then eventually birthed into the world.

Herein lies the evidence for The Balance Theory.

Nature is showing us, in every cycle, season and transition, that we were born with the innate pull towards equilibrium. That beauty exists in the search for the balance. That we are equal parts *this* and *that*.

The summer is delicious because winter holds the internal warmth.

Seasons are imperative in life's circle.

In the past five years especially, we have started to answer this call globally. As a collective, we have moved into a time where pride is now validated as a socially just movement—albeit a few decades late, but better late than never.

We are starting to wake up to the idea that every human being of every race, orientation, gender and ethnicity is permitted and should be *allowed* their universal birthright to explore the equal parts of their feminine and masculine qualities.

Masculine and feminine traits exist within us all—no matter the sex or gender you were physically and biologically born into.

As we move through this discussion, it is important to note that we are speaking to the attributes of energy that presents as either more 'masculine' or more 'feminine' in nature. This essentially means that it doesn't matter what your genitalia presents as; you are only truly balanced when you can recognise that both sides of the coin exist within you.

The overview is this:

1. Masculine energetics refers to vibration that is responsive to structure, discipline, order and command. If it were a shape, the masculine would be linear and representative of goal direction. The achiever. The breadwinner. The action-oriented type. The masculine is culturally depicted as the sun for this reason—daytime equals time to work hard and kick goals. The masculine helps to get sh*t done. The masculine is Yang energy at its core.

2. Feminine energetics are those that allow for softening. She nurtures. She tells you that it will 'all be okay'. She is intuitively creative. When the feminine shows up authentically in the context of a female body, in most cases, she can literally take that creative fire and grow a human being. It is the same creative power that runs through us all that provides inspiration and innovation. The feminine is whimsical. In a male body, she is the constant reminder that softening is a form of authentic human expression. She gives birth to empathy.
   > She isn't afraid of darkness.
   > She finds rest in cool, dark spaces.
   > If she were a shape, she'd be circular.

   Unity.
   Womb shape.
   She is play.

> She is the moon providing glow for the most restful sleep at night. She is Yin energy. She asks you to show up naked, raw and in truth.

As a human being, you possess and express both qualities. The voice of the balance whispers this sacred wisdom on the subject:

Denying either the Divine Masculine or Feminine will hurt you. And by you, I mean collective You.
To the human race: you've been hurting for a long time. Your masculine wounds have bled all over the feminine. She could no longer tell where her own bleed started and where it stopped. Her sacred month has been in pain for years, millennia even. It is time to cry, to bleed together.

Despite the 'womanly' and voluptuous curvature that is my physical body, my mind grew up masculine. After years of soul searching and a deep dive into the ancestral psyche that was handed down to me from my lineage, this (now) comes as no surprise to me. Both sets of my grandparents are Italian immigrants who came to Australia in search of 'the good life' post World War II. Scarcity mindset and working hard for the dollar were literally carved into my DNA before I decided to come earthside—and for good reason. The incessant need to provide for family—to forage and safeguard for the future—is an extremely masculine trait. Every time I run my business accounts for the month, I hear my nonna's voice bounce around in my head.

'Always save for the rainy day.'

While doing deep psychological work on myself enmeshed with months of body mapping in preparation to fall pregnant, it became apparent to me that while my grandparents (and to an extent, my parents) needed to 'hustle' to literally survive, I was fortunate enough to not need to have my nervous system respond from scarcity and lack any more.

My body and my mind were not war torn and yet, my nervous system was behaving like they were. My cells, my thoughts, my actions were united by the same belief that to 'drop the ball' when it came to work and finances was irresponsible and unacceptable.

Something was missing, and it turned out that that something was my feminine.

The part of me that delighted in 'fun'. The part of myself that enjoyed tap dancing and laughing out loud hysterically had been shut off for a good while.

The part of me that knew the power of my sensual worth was completely barren.

My menstrual cycle was directly subjected to the disarray that was occurring frequently throughout my adolescence and early twenties. My cells were screaming, *Come home to us, Tash!*

My mind was elsewhere.

My body went with it.

Emotions? Well they were well and truly denied and buried heavily under a festering lump of shame.

Hormonally, my feminine decided it was time to tap out

and go offline for a while. Years of irregular bleeds and overall feminine absence became my reality.

What was the point in having a natural cycle, ready to create life, if the life that was hosting at the time was dishonouring its truth?

I was lacking and so was she.

I was hiding and so was she.

I was MIA and so was my bleed.

She didn't feel like nurturing and neither did I.

So she and I decided (mutually) not to show up for our monthly meeting.

My masculine was not impressed, to say the least.

Depression will do that to you. The darkness takes the body-mind-spirit motivators and numbs them to a point of dysfunction. For a woman, her cycle and its health (or lack thereof) is a telltale indicator of overall wellbeing over a month's period. It's an in-built feminine KPI tracker, and yet the irony of feminine energy is that she doesn't respond to 'order' or specific goal setting.

That's all for the patriarchy.

That's all for the masculine.

As part of the natural systems that run freely on Earth, our wellbeing needs equality to function.

Yin must meet Yang.

Darkness, light.

Happiness can only be known when true sadness is deeply felt.

Black and white are equal shades on the same plane.

Masculine energy only thrives when feminine energy is nurtured

When a soul is balanced, it is free to express the masculine and feminine openly and without judgement. Anything less than this expression results in dissonance. In extreme cases, it can result in the loss of life. Unfortunately, there are too many stories that exist, especially in the queer community, of gorgeous beings becoming subjected to their own mental torture, acts of self-harm and, more tragically, suicidal tendencies and behaviours due to a lifetime of denying the manner in which they choose to express their divinity. Just the other day, two of my dearest friends in the queer community posted the same message on Instagram that read, *Queer people don't grow up ourselves.*

The message smacked me square in the face. The words, so icy in their delivery. And ultimately, this is true. Many beautiful beings of the rainbow have had no choice but to live a very dicey youth pained by fear and coated in dishonesty.

Hearts—broken.

First and foremost by loved ones, and often, the family unit, let alone their significant others.

We are all here to dance with the divine.

When we are considered by society to be heteronormative and cisgendered, we don't have to fight for the expression in the dance sequence. We simply have to place one foot in front of the other and the audience applauds us. The choreography is not complicated and is very easy on the eye. It makes us feel *comfortable.* When we dance the steps the way we have been socially conditioned to, and find the seemingly perfect partner of the opposite sex to lead or follow accordingly, generations before us feel at ease. Our queer counterparts are left to fumble through, feeling as though having two left feet is synonymous with being less than desirable.

It is just simply not true.

It never has been, and yet, historically, we really have all mastered the skill of denying the beauty of the rainbow.

Our collective rainbow; too many shades of grey to be fully seen and accepted.

Allow me to continue to share the beauty in Mitch's story—one of the brightest shades of grey in my life.

8 January 2015

> *It felt right.*
> *To grab your hand in mine and to lay by your side.*
> *I had held you and you held me.*
> *And we were raw.*
> *You have helped me to articulate Friendship.*
>
> *You are True.*
> *You are Being.*
> *And*
> *Beautiful.*
>
> *I wanted to hold your vulnerability for infinite time and space.*

I wanted to watch you glue your jigsaw pieces together.

I say watch because—
You.
Me.

We are observers.
We watch things.

Incessantly watching.
We watch and understand.
We pick it up with our fingers and pull apart the pieces—
Examine the nth degree of possibility.
And in doing so,
We make sense of it.

And in this moment now,
We are scientists and quantifiers.

Do you think we know what we are doing?

Do you think we've observed it yet?
Our place,
In This Space.

We are learners and teachers.
We fuel one another.

Highly charged stories, running off
Electric Energy.

We educate our souls.

Last night,
Together;
We achieved quietness of the night mind.
A sense of alleviating
The Weight we all feel.
Combined,
Just us two
And then later,
Collectively.
On a larger scale.

I know and you know that we're going to defy the fifth dimension
Together,
Wherever that may be.

A pact to travel,
Because last night,
We were truly free.

This poem signifies for me one of the deepest experiences of human empathy I have ever been privileged enough to feel. It poured out of me effortlessly, after the emotional resonance of that night continued to pervade my space for weeks on end.

It was the middle of summer. We had just left the cinema after watching *Interstellar*—both fascinated by questions of our place here on Earth and the meaning behind it all; Mitch and me, both fans of exploring quite literally what is extraterrestrial and how that plays out in our 3D world. We were obsessed, to say the least.

We were high off the discussion of the cinematography of the film. Nerding out together on this stuff had been a recent pastime of ours. Our friendship was in its youth as we had met at a music festival only five months before. There was so much anticipation with our meeting, though. For years prior, we had been operating in each other's circles and had a bunch of friends in common—but had not yet formally crossed paths. At the time, Mitch was somewhat 'involved' with one of my best girlfriends, Alex.

At heart, Mitch is a true Travelling Partner of mine; a term you'll come to know from Chapter 6 onwards. 'Travelling Partner' is the term coined with you here and now to describe the most intense level of soul connection you can possibly encounter. Our bond was inevitable from that night onwards.

His car was our cocoon and the eventual secret keeper for the night.

It was well and truly after midnight when he dropped me off at home. Mitch is an extremely vibrant soul and it serves him well. It's the reason he collects people from all walks of life and makes enough room on the shelf for each individual, ensuring they don't have an expiry date. I love this about him and it's likely because this part of him is a direct mirror of how I choose to live my own life.

This particular evening, he was laser focused.

Mitch is as skilful a wordsmith as he is charming. His charisma will keep you hanging on every word. Midnight turned to 1:00 am, then shortly 2:00 am, bordering 3:00 am.

Time was bending over into that territory that is only ever reserved for existential crises, making art, making love, or participating in taboo or illegal activity, if not asleep.

As I went to say goodbye and head inside, I could feel the tension in the space.

It was palpable and unnerving.

I had two immediate thoughts.

First, my then boyfriend (now husband, Vince) was backpacking Tokyo. I needed to get to bed so I could get up and Facetime him tomorrow before work. The intensity in our space was threatening.

Second—*You're involved with Alex.* Nothing had necessarily 'happened' and yet the innocence of a three-hour parked car chat was feeling like a line had been crossed.

Just as I was about to open the car door and sink deep into my sheets, Mitch reached over and grabbed my hand.

He really grabbed it. He squeezed it.

(He did not let go of it for an hour thereafter.)

He opened his mouth, and closed it again.

Blood was violently pulsing through our veins. His grip was so tight; I could not tell if I was feeling my own physical rhythm or if it was his.

Then, silence.

Just pulsing.

Now, reaching my ears.

Pounding in my head.

I had no idea what I was anticipating but Mitch had calculated this very moment. He had probably rehearsed and conducted this moment in his head, over and over, his whole life.

Then he spoke, his voice broken; the mirror of his heart.

'Tash, I am in love.'

I looked him dead in the eye and told him I was too. That I could not wait for Vince to come home …

Then—

Silence again, both our eyes on our white-knuckle grip.

'His name is Jay.'

Immediately, a thousand breaths in one.

Head, spinning. Mind calculating. I squeezed his hand tighter.

'His?'

His eyes were crying, but the tears had not caught up yet.

I processed it.

The only words I managed came out next.

'How long … what about Alex? … Who knows?'

'No one. Just you.'

We spoke for hours.

Hours went for days.

We continued to speak for weeks.

Months.

Years.

Mitch had years of lying to himself to unpack, declutter and rearrange. The biggest life lesson he endured was the art of The Divine Dance. Harsh learnings that came with denying his truth—a truth he had known from childhood—came hard and fast soon after that night.

The significance of recognising masculinity and femininity in the shape of queerness soon became clear to me again. Only two days after Mitch came out to me, my other soul brother, Joey, took his turn and bared his soul.

Holding Joey's hand while he honoured his truth, I allowed him to play with my hair, freeing his feminine by equally holding my space. The capacity to hold space, even when his own has felt morose, is Joey's purest gift to the world. When depression was the projection in my barbed mind, Joey was the holder of my torch—a light I've been lucky enough to bathe in abundantly. To see him unapologetically free in his own right was to bear witness to true, human integrity.

Later that year, Australian same-sex marriage laws were passed. My femme cried all of the tears that day. Finally, the political realisation that at the heart of it all, leadership—traditionally a masculine paradigm—would be socially *safest* when governed by the feminine heart. Intrinsically, human bodies express both the masc and femme uniquely. The balance of both equates to measured health. How this expression manifests across mind, body and spirit is ultimately irrelevant.

As long as the bipolarities have come to fruition, then Universe's goal is met.

And yet, the two energies are not necessarily *gendered*. Ironically, and even in the context of this chapter, to gender the masculine or the feminine is dangerous.

It encourages a very conditioned and out-of-touch fallacy.

It sends mixed messages to the kids.

The confusion tips the scales into a territory that is hard to recalibrate as time goes on.

Regardless of our path, our purpose requires both masculine and feminine qualities to be fully functioning so that our light can come through. Shame on either side of the scale is not conducive to a successful life. Denial in this space is tantamount to mental and emotional illness.

For Mitch, he had always been a beautiful gay man sporting a very masculine mask. It was too rigid, too angular, for the delicacy that was his spirit.

Eventually, the mask would hurt people, but not as much as it hurt himself.

It landed him in hospital.

Twice, over the five years thereafter.

He had no choice but to drop the battle and own *all* of it.

His diagnosis, bipolar.

Sick from denying the most gracious bipolarity of them all—the divine dance of the masc and femme.

Mitch's masculine, so unnaturally, had to retreat so that his feminine could uncharacteristically strike. His feminine was fierce. Fuelled by years of pent-up masculine rage.

To this day, one of the most precious events I've ever witnessed was the week that both Mitch and Joey, unbeknownst to one another, came home to themselves.

Grit to glitter.

All fragments of the same.

Grey—

Gold.

The gold that is both their hearts.

The lesson

Our lesson here is so simple.

The individual and the collective must learn to take the masculine and teach that energy to hold femininity.

That is the greatest challenge in the mission for balance.

The natural state of human order will be restored when this truly comes to fruition. Historically, our race has completely missed this piece, hurting many souls in the process because of a patriarchy so headstrong, it's been blinded by its own light.

If we look outside of ourselves, we will come to realise that the answers have been there all along. The sanctity within this wisdom is as old as the sun making way for the moon to heal and the moon respecting that the sun's fate was always to shine.

Balanced bipolarities give space for truth, authenticity.

Consciousness expressing consciousness.

The Divine Dance.

Questions for your soul work

1
What is your current relationship with masculine energy?

2
What is your current relationship with feminine energy?

3
Is there anything you need to heal at either end of the spectrum?

4
Is your 'dance' divine at the moment? What actions/practices bring the energy into alignment for you?

5

How do both masculine and feminine energies present in your physical body, your psyche and your emotional body? Are there equal parts ebb and flow present in your life?

6

What would it mean to surrender to the masculine?

7

What would it mean to surrender to the feminine?

8

What inspired action do you receive from the natural world?

CHAPTER 6

Travelling Partners

The Lesson: Our connections prepare us for the ultimate surrender.

Kindling: The birth of Travelling Partners

When I met my boyfriend (now husband) in 2005, at the age of fourteen, I knew I would marry him.

Like, truly, in the depth of my core, I just *knew*.

Later one evening (more like early morning before needing to get up for school), Vincent typed over MSN messenger the words that every teenage girl has romanticised at some point in their youth (cue message alert tone that resides in the back of every Millennial's head).

Will you marry me?

Before I had a chance to type back my big, hormonally driven *YES!*—in fine teenage-boy form—that heart-stopping one liner was followed up with a *nah, just kidding.*

Embarrassed on the other end of the screen, trying to keep my cool, I waited.

He typed back after a long five minutes: *Well not really kidding, but I am for today. I do mean it though. One day, I will ask you that question and you will say yes and it'll be the start of the strongest marriage ever known.*

Naive and pure—yes.

But damn.

He was right.

I couldn't wipe the smile off my face that day. It is the same smile that coated all of our wedding photos ten years after that fateful conversation and the same one that I wore the day our son was born last year. The smile of knowing for certain that I was with the most important man in my life and that I chose to *choose* him every day from that moment forth.

Through many conversations along the grapevine, and due to the number of people interwoven in our worlds, we are almost certain that we met as children. Four-year-olds, playing kickball out the back of my aunty's kiosk. In the community we grew up in, soccer games were like a mini festival every weekend. So naturally, between pizza carts, gelato vans and the kiosk, every child in a five-kilometre radius would gravitate towards the food stands while their parents either participated in or spectated the soccer.

Our story was not to intertwine until we 'met' again at fourteen years old, in high school. As all good stories would have it, our forced friendship commenced when we were placed in a seating arrangement based on surname. Both of our surnames beginning with P meant that not only were we seated together, but we were positioned awkwardly as a pair, which forced us to complete assessment tasks and sit exams together.

At school, we were literally from different worlds. Me, the academic overachiever and socially well rounded. I could befriend anyone and everyone from the gatekeeper to an outcast peer. Vincent belonged to the underground world of the 'emo kids'—a group I liked to dabble in and out of in the safe space of my music class, but definitely not during lunchtime. I had social justice meetings to attend and debating competitions to chair.

Our somewhat coerced union at the hands of our teachers and their rules felt like… kismet. There was a palpable chemistry that fired down my spine when we would accidentally drop a pencil and have to reach over each other's imaginary boundary line to pick it up. We shared that desk for many years.

At the time, I couldn't quite interpret why I was so energetically drawn to him. Over time, whenever I'd see his face or hear his name, I would feel a burning sensation in the pit of my stomach. Over the years, I would come to learn that this sensation was my body's natural way of housing my intuition and bringing it to my conscious awareness.

I would seek out opportunities just to talk about him.

I'd plan a scenario so that I would have to engage with him—outside the context of our classroom seating arrangement.

Initially, it definitely wasn't a crush.

I knew what *that* felt like.

This was rawer and certainly more *appealing*.

It was discombobulating. I was addicted to the idea of being in and around his energy field.

At. all. times.

Eventually, Vincent would start to show up in my dreams. He began entering my world from both conscious and unconscious ends of the spectrum.

And that was just it. I had heard at the time the idea that if someone was on your mind, then perhaps they were *supposed* to be there.

I didn't know it at the time, but essentially, the concept of the Travelling Partner was starting to plant somewhere in my unconscious field. I was quite often experiencing a visceral response somewhere in my solar plexus at the sheer presence or simple mention of Vincent. What manifested eventually was me sharing his last name. The same name that placed me next to him on the desk, all those years ago.

My body just *knew*. My soul was speaking to me through my vessel—this boy was important. My heart exploded for him before I even really got to know him.

Somewhere in his cells was the genetic imprint for my son. Intuition gave me permission to deeply sense that. Our chemistry was so magnetic, we didn't need to consult the textbook. Talk about a covalent bond.

The connection I felt to Vincent was unlike anything I had experienced before. It was my first real insight into the idea of feeling attached to something bigger than myself or my immediate world. Sure, I had definitely felt love and safety in the confines of my family, especially my immediate circle, but I guess this was the first time that I was consciously tapping into soul-level union beyond my then teenage comprehension. I was aware of the idea of 'destiny' and certainly its place in every Hollywood film I'd seen to that point, but this connection came with a *hunger*.

For the first time in my life, there was a bottomless union. It was forming first and foremost within myself but it was naturally extending an energetic olive branch to *Other*.

His heart and his heartbreak, I wanted it all.

His happiness was mine.

Mine was his.

His pain was mine. I *shared* it. I went there.

I *was* there.

All the way.

My most favourite possession was his t-shirt and I wore it under my clothes just to feel him around no matter where I was.

It truly was the 'all or nothing' feeling.

We took 'ride or die' to the nth degree and revelled in that idea together.

We took pleasure in the pain, together.

There is nothing quite like being with someone for an extended period of time. In the thirteen years we've been together since, my greatest joys and deepest sorrows are synonymous with his …

But this is not a chapter about love-struck teens and the Hollywood ideation of 'soulmates'.

It is *more* than that.

While I am a firm believer in the concept of fate, in channelling this work, I politely request permission to completely destroy that story, even though my personal story is one that fits that classic, lovesick romantic mould.

We live in a world where stories of 'knowing' that you've met The One are not uncommon. Most of our experience of film, music and art dramatises and romanticises the very concept that there is one person out there for anyone who has ever walked the planet.

Right here and now, I'd love to break your heart, on purpose—to crack it wide open and explore the possibility that you, my dear reader, have multiple people of importance who are more than destined to walk in and out of your life over the course of your divine lifetime. Significantly, in fact, your 'Ones' are often *not* your romantic or sexual partner. Sure, it is a given that a significant other is sure as hell a Travelling Partner, but they are not the only one.

This is a venture into the idea of significant *others*—the others that are so heavily intertwined with our soul's purpose.

One day, Vincent and I were lying in bed, holding each other and revelling in our post-lovemaking haze.

Time was at a standstill.

There was nothing more profound in that moment than that blissed-out state.

The silence was medicine.

And then, he leant over and kissed me on the forehead, as he always did.

'Do you believe there is more than one person out there for us in this lifetime?' he asked in a tone that was somewhere between a question and a 'matter of fact' statement.

'Like … as in, a soulmate?'

'Kind of …' he trailed off.

I answered hard and fast.

'Absolutely not. To think there is someone that could replace you, us, in this moment … ludicrous.' I smiled it off, lighthearted and good natured. I expected him to follow suit with my sentiment.

'I do.'

'Do what …?' I began, already fully aware of where this conversation was going.

'I do believe that we could replace each other.' He proceeded to roll over and do up his pants; so nonchalant, my Vincent. He loved to drop an oral bomb with no desire to clean up the debris. He was so sure of himself like that.

I stared at the roof. A tear streaming down my eye.

HOW DARE HE.

How dare he suggest that the uniqueness of our connection was *disposable*.

How dare he allude to the idea that our love was *randomised*.

Suffice to say, at the time, our love was so fired up, it was ignited by unkempt embers.

Pristine, egocentric veneration.

I was not to know it yet, but that conversation and the heart-stopping fury that followed met me *exactly* where I needed to be.

In the months to come, that conversation would become the unconscious backbone that flipped the script on my entire outlook on life: how I would come to perceive new people, how I would eventually come to teach others of the raw beauty that was the tinder of true soul connection.

The journey with Vincent has in fact taught me the consequence of true imbalance. Imbalance of any sort in the name of love, while beautiful, has the capacity to be completely vain. It is literally choosing one side of the camp and setting up without any consideration for any other possibility.

Our energy together outweighed anything else of importance in life for a fair portion of my early twenties. While this ideal is more romantic than a Nicholas Sparks novel, it can be detrimental to the health of a relationship. Psychologically, this is the manifestation of codependency. Codependency takes the 'I can't live without you' notion and turns it into disarray.

The odyssey from codependence to true interdependence with Vincent is, to this day, one of my greatest achievements. And I share the trophy with him, standing by his side. Over the past thirteen years, we have exchanged dysfunctional late nights at bars for wedding vows and promised to be each other's *Other* for as long as we both shall live.

The irony is though, we both understand now more than ever before that we don't possess one another. We don't even regard one another as capable of being possessed because we realise in the most wholesome and deliberate way that as sentient beings, in liberating each other, we are truly free.

A life partner is the conscious choice to make a Travelling Partner an earthside companion for life.

We have now crossed the intersection of this theory. The point where conceptually, balance resides outside the context of the individual and begins to energetically dance with 'Other'. The bottom line is that the concept of balance itself is best measured when two individuals, as two separate vessels, collaborate in unison with one another. As a species, we are literally wired to want to be together.

We *desire* balance in partnership.

That togetherness is most functional when a completely connected individual intertwines with their Other who is also aligned within Self.

That alignment lights the soul on fire.

Enter the discussion on soul connection in relationships.

More specifically, the question and the mystery of 'soul connection'.

As I was channelling these pages—and particularly, this concept—soul connection entered my consciousness with a very specific name: Travelling Partners. And with it, a very specific visualisation.

Two people, holding hands and walking into the abyss of a Universal vortex.

These two souls representing the dichotomy of balance in itself.

One Yin, one Yang.

Essentially, the notion that we are walking—*travelling*, if you will—with our soul counterparts throughout lifetimes.

Time and time again, I have found myself in situations that I call by the name of Fate. Moments with my lover, my child, a new friend, an old friend, my siblings, my parents, my clients. The people I feel I've known for 'all of eternity'.

There is a reason this concept feels universal—because *it is* universal.

There is no greater pleasure than sharing Travelling Partners with you all. My hope for you, my reader, is that you are able to identify your own Travelling Partners and the place they have in your life. A deeper gratitude for their presence is the only outcome that matters after entertaining this idea with me. So, let's go back to the beginning of this download and unpack the Universal wisdom that prevailed thereafter.

Season, reason, lifetime

People are in your life for a season, a reason or a lifetime. This statement is commonly thrown around as a buzz phrase, especially in spiritual circles. In its simplicity, I wholeheartedly subscribe to it. As someone who expresses nothing but utter joy when meeting someone new, I definitely belong to the camp that enjoys placing the person in front of me into one of those three categories.

It fits. It's neat.

It allows me to meet everyone with a gracious appreciation for their presence—even in the event that I haven't gelled well with them upon first meeting.

In a freezing-cold Swiss hotel room, the first download about the idea of a Travelling Partner started to emerge. I was in my early twenties and had, along with four other best mates, set out to explore every corner of mainland Europe, as all good Millennials did. We squeezed our voyage between semesters. The channelling of The Balance Theory hadn't entered my consciousness yet, but the idea that the people I had just met were part of a story larger than my life to date was mind blowing.

Mid-July 2012—Florence, Italy

She didn't know what she needed,
But it definitely wasn't him.
Together, they didn't have answers, they weren't trying to
'fix' anything.
They were subtle like that.
When they couldn't find words,
They'd find walks.
Put their fingers on the map
And they'd go there.
Destination unknown,
But they were coming home.
To all ends of the earth,
By foot and by mind.
The realisation of each other was beyond
This Lifetime.
With him she found,
More than ever before,
Unshakable intuition
It was Fem, it was wounded, ultimately raw.
In trusting that he taught her,
There was no greater power than trust in Self.
Somewhere between Berlin and Prague,
She was shown that
The Soul speaks in Foreign Tongue.

I woke up with this download hot on my mind after a very intense dream. The dream followed a night of partying and gallivanting around Piazza Santa Croce in Florence. It featured two very curious people.

You know that feeling in a dream where you know it is *you* and you're almost certain that you know the other person, but they kind of look different?

One of those dreams.

The other person in the dream was my new-found friend, Tom, who I met on day one of our European adventure. We were a fresh ten days into knowing each other. Our friends were beginning to play 'mix and match' and our worlds were colliding at rapid speed. Days knowing each other felt equal to years on that trip …

But the dream suggested otherwise.

In essence, we had had a conversation.

A very lucid dream about having met in another lifetime.

I cannot confirm to you, my reader, whether this dream actually held any *weight*, but it planted a very fertile seed.

And didn't that seed germinate.

Tom would end up introducing me to new-age paradigms, the documentary series, *Zeitgeist* and all the fun things between. He was one of the first people to truly test my world view, in all the right ways. He held up a mirror to allow me to fully see myself through many hours of conversation.

Cut to real-time human experience, and Tom and I were bonding over a common love for Oasis's 'Wonderwall' and melancholic indie films. Agreeing that *Midnight in Paris* was nothing short of a masterpiece, we set out to walk from one end of Paris to the other in a night to visit the key sites of the film. We definitely achieved that goal, stopping at every cafe for a crepe, coffee or foreign delicacy along the way for fuel. We collected friends on our journey, which ended at some ungodly hour in front of the Eiffel Tower.

I took a breath and inhaled the essence around me.

I was in my favourite city. With a collection of my favourite people. Some I had known for my entire life, some I felt I had known for *lifetimes*.

My fellow *travellers*.

My Travelling Partners.

It landed instantaneously for me.

Surely, kismet connection was universal?

It simply wasn't explainable in logical, linear terms, so I concluded that it had to be.

Immediately, I thought back to the moment in bed with Vince …

There was one hundred per cent room for multiple soul counterparts, because I had just integrated with mine.

August 2012—two weeks after returning home

The simplicity of admiring the person standing in front of you.

Travelling forced me to believe that every single person you encounter in life is a stepping stone towards a better version of you. Some of those stones 'skim your surface' and before you get to explore the deeper waters with them, they've moved on in the ripple effect we call 'Life'. Some of those stones turn into the bedrock that forms your foundation, concretely knowing who you are and keeping your waters still when you need a sense of calm …

Ultimately, you are travelling this world alone, but we are vital to one another. Whether it was that brief encounter on a train, or the conversation that started over coffee and grew into a friendship, the circumstance remains the same.

We're all just moving forward.

People and Places, what a romantic union.

Weeks after landing on home soil, the bigger questions around meeting certain people were beginning to emerge. What I had experienced in Europe only a month prior—undeniable human connection with perfect 'strangers'—formed a new train of obsessive thinking in my overactive mind.

Had I met these people for a season? Was it okay to let the season fall away and give rise to a new one? What would that look like?

Had we met for a reason? If so, what was the point in that level of emotional depth and personal investment for no longer than a month or so?

A lifetime? Did these new-found souls hold more for me beyond the whimsical world of our trip?

More to the point: if we walk this life and 'bump in and out' of Travelling Partner relationships, what is the Universal goal for that taking place?

Existentialism at its finest.

And ever more so in the next statement.

Why, if people are supposed to stick around for their Universally assigned reason, season or lifetime, would Universe rip people away from you, seemingly before what would be considered their given earthly time?

Why did people like my dear husband have to endure a soul-destroying level of emotional turmoil with the loss of a best friend so young in life?

Six months later, in between my dream state and twangs of early morning meditation, another download. This stream came through after a night of sipping tea with my beautiful friend, Lucy. We were obsessing over the awe of travelling. We shared our bug together. I was (still) ruminating on the magic of my European lessons while she outlined, in specific detail, her pull towards the echoes of Indian wanderlust.

Probably the most profound download dropped in for me that fateful morning:

Universally, there is a pull towards the balance of soul energy.

Any given soul in your life right now has been specifically placed there.

The soul—the one that is taking up so much space in your present reality, the one/s occupying your mental capacity as you process this statement—may be a product of a karmic 'hangover' from a previous version of Self. An alternate timeline or perhaps a new karmic line in this lifetime, to be carried over to the next.

Trust in this process. This is Universal guidance in action.

Once the soul-by-soul connection has exercised its lesson or assignment, Universe will perform very simple yet precise energetic mathematics.

The physical reality may either keep that soul in one's conscious field, or subtract it, but the energetic union is unable to be destroyed. That vibrational line connecting two souls, and potentially more, is pure cosmic energy.

That line is made of the same oneness that gives the tree its seasonal fate and links the moon to her tides.

Suspend the timeline; it is not important.

It is meaningless because when we only have conscious access to the Earthly timeline, we are privy only to the human form. When a soul has touched another soul, that energetic union is eternal. There are times when Universe requires the energetic 'weight' of a specific soul makeup, beyond its Earthly existence.
This is the human experience of 'death'.

The soul must transcend beyond this realm and move through to the next to ensure Universal balance is maintained Elsewhere.

That is why it hurts: because you don't fully understand this yet.

The hurt is human.

It is raw and painful but the Universal motivator for death is so much more than what you're tapped into.
This is your permission to tap in.

The experience of death in this reality is the preservation of life in another. Universally, we are immortalised because of the experience that is pure soul connection.

The soul connections placed on your path for your specific soul journey are your Travelling Partners. In travelling through life(times) with you, they are the containers for you to spill your lessons into. They mirror back to you in forms of light and shade.

Their existence is your colour spectrum and you are theirs.

A 'soulmate' is always a Travelling Partner, but not all Travelling Partners are soulmates. Soulmates are just that: mates that your soul chooses to oscillate with.
You have a conscious choice over whether or not to keep the soulmate around.

A Travelling Partner has something very unique, because they hold a fragment of you. Your essence becomes the souvenir in the story of their travels. But there is something very specific about your Travelling Partners—and this is the distinction, the 'how you know you've met one': A Travelling Partner in Earthly form has experienced heartbreak either with you, from you or for you. The heartbreak comes from two halves of the same core.

You each hold a piece.
Because halves are balanced.

From that point on, the manifesto for Travelling Partners became the framework by which I chose to articulate any experience that had the capacity to make me feel out of body. It has been there for me in any given circumstance that has pushed me to the upper limit of unwavering faith.

Travelling Partners has allowed me to bury one too many souls in my life taken prematurely, by earthly standards.

Travelling Partners has taught me that I can be *in love* and *deeply love Other*, simultaneously.

Travelling Partners has enabled me to part with dear friends when the timing was required for our boundaries to be truly respected by one another.

Travelling Partners has given me the gracious gift of gratitude for my family, who I choose to keep as friends, and my friends who are so deeply imprinted in my DNA, they are my family.

Further, Travelling Partners gives me the mercy to accept the place of those in my life who haven't held the best of intentions. They were the direct teachers that guided me straight back to my own self-worth.

A Travelling Partner is the truest reflector of your soul.

Travelling Partners make the fulcrum of life functional.

A Travelling Partner union is Universal balance in action.

It keeps us going.

Follow the (unconscious) crumbs

If heartbreak (with, from or for you) is a defining feature of the Travelling Partner relationship, then there is another universal law that comes within that union.

The unconscious crumbs.

If the relationship is a truth for you to experience in this lifetime, ask your unconscious mind. It will show you, in its very cryptic language of sign and symbol, the answers to any questions you may have about the Other in question, especially when the relationship manifests over rough waters.

The unconscious crumbs—and the modalities by which they choose to come through—express uniquely for us all.

Throughout my life, my crumbs have been fed to me threefold.

In dreams.

In meditations.

In childhood memories.

For some people, it may be in deja vu moments.

Or in the state of flow that prevails when making art.

Or making food.

Or making love.

Or when taking plant medicine, if that's what you choose.

Or when numbers, signs or patterns happen to drop into your conscious field without your *conscious permission*.

Or when dates align.

Or when nouns take on a rather imperative role beyond their grammatical constructs.

People, places and things that appear in serendipitous timing.

Think Gwyneth Paltrow in *Sliding Doors* but know that the door is always going to be the one for you in real time because you are co-creating every relationship, lesson and actuality with Universe.

Trust that your soul essence will allow you to see it all when your highest evolvement *requires* that for you.

The realisation that the crumb was in fact a crumb often occurs outside the context of the real-time moment.

There is nothing else here except pervading Universal trust.

The crumb will come when you are required by Universe to *integrate* it into your linear reality.

It's a spiritual muscle that we all have the choice to activate—or not.

That is where free will comes in.

It's in your power.

Go as far as you need to go with your lesson.

The let-go

As prominent as a first meeting with a Travelling Partner is, so is the experience of coming to terms within Self that the 'travelling', for the time being, has been done. You'll recall from Chapter 4 that we introduced the notion of Energy Expired.

Energy Expired and Travelling Partners knocked on my energetic door in the same year. I was reconciling grief that came from massive shifts in friendship dynamics post Dylan's death. Vincent and I watched people literally walk in and out of our lives at rapid speed. We had no choice but to pay attention to it because our reality was not the same pre and post my Europe trip.

We found ourselves officially at the intersection of grief.

Grief for the dead.

Grief for the living.

Truth be told, grieving for the person who was still living and choosing by circumstance to leave my life felt *harder* to 'do' at that point in time. Grief for the living often yields mental unrest— that is, relentless mental unrest because the wound is perpetually open. The gaping emptiness invites a sad concept of 'unrealised possibility', which can propagate grief further.

Death is masterful in presenting you with a finite answer. A physical 'this is where it ends for you and the *other*'.

But a Travelling Partner leaving your physical reality while they continue to exist, with their significant others … energetically, it *expires you*.

We have no choice but to find comfort in the quantum

truth that energy cannot be created or destroyed. Rather, for the current reality in question, the soul connection for the linear world has been suspended and the two souls in question continue to travel—apart.

Onwards and upwards and off to fill an energetic void—elsewhere.

If you multiply the amount of expired energetic connections by the exponential combinations of human connections, one at a time, on this planet, the equation would balance itself out.

Energy expires so that soul connection continues to wire. It takes the notion of 'six degrees of separation' and elevates that beyond our 3D world.

That energy transcends the human experience and allows us to contact reality ever-present.

A physical let-go is an energetic infinity symbol.

There is an importance in realising a very crucial and ironic step in the material 'let go' process: with the intention to 'let go', you'll never fully void a tie because the memory, the essence of that person, of that soul, is hyper-present in your energetic imprint.

When the connection with a Travelling Partner is pure, wholesome and true, it feeds love.

All pointing back to you.

Teaching you how to self-love.

A just union. Harmonious.

That's how you know—you've met your mirror in that moment.

When in a Travelling Partner relationship—

The need to be seen leads to being seen.

The need to be held leads to being held.
The need to be felt leads to being touched.
The need to be looked after and to look after—
Is Achieved.

The lesson

The ultimate lesson here is this: you can sever the tie, cut the cord, bid farewell (or whatever term lands for you), but essentially, your Travelling Partners build you into the person you are today, ever travelling with the common light source that brought the two of you together in the first place. That is the sheer reason your true Travelling Partner, whether presently living or past, has a piece of you, and you a piece of them.

Whether in this lifetime or the next, you'll arrive back at the place where you were meant to meet, and resolve the karmic forces that exist between your ties. This is the Universe playing puppet master and that is absolutely perfect and okay.

Just send love and the intention of true connection.
You've shown up and played your part.

Until then, surrender is enough.
Surrender is survival and—
Moving on.

Enter next Travelling Partner, enter new lessons.
Evolution.

Questions for your soul work

1

Who are your Travelling Partners? Write them down on a page and have their names really clear. Reflect on each person and the role they have had or continue to have in your life.

2

What lessons have you learned because of your Travelling Partners?

3

What lessons have you integrated because of your Travelling Partners?

4

Can you practise a new level of gratitude simply by knowing who your Travelling Partners are? How will you do this?

5
How does the Energy Expired concept sit with you now, in the context of Travelling Partners?

6
Are there some conversations you need to have with some of your past or current Travelling Partners? If yes, how will you honour this need to communicate with them?

7
What does surrendering a Travelling Partner relationship mean to you?

8
Are the relationships you have with your current Travelling Partners experiencing a phase of balance or imbalance? If applicable, what does 'letting go' look like in this space?

CHAPTER 7

Navigating Adversity

The Lesson: A life without adversity is a life imbalanced.

Necessity

The lesson is simple. We start this chapter at its end.

Which points us back to that full-circle notion.

Universe is not concerned with whether or not the play was *fair*. What does that even mean anyway? We are fated to walk alongside adversity; the ultimate teacher in this lifetime. It is the one guarantee.

Universe knows balance in giving us cards to make our play. We don't know the endgame. We don't know how it's destined to finish or even how long we will be playing for. The cards are being revealed to us one at a time. We make our decisions based on the *safety* of the previous play. We remain poker faced because we often can't pre-empt the next move. Even if we wanted to.

Adversity is dealt on a needs basis—PRN on the soul's orders.

The other day, I questioned the opposite of unconditional love. I figured that the answer to that must be unconditional pain. To that end, the *unconditional* component is just that.

Sometimes, there are no conditions. Human pain is there to

be *felt*. In a weird way, the pain holds us close and can transmute us back to our grounding.

Pain has a way of keeping us idle until we have no choice other than to face its root cause.

In that space, we need to ground, to go back to the drawing board so that we can rebirth.

The following chapter is a collection of stories that reveal the full circle. Examples of balance fighting for its place. Positives and negatives have no place here.

The shadow in the eclipse is worth a look in.

We're not broken, just bent
October 2015. Rehabilitation ward, level four.

I nervously approached her as she sat so helplessly in her bed.

Pristine whiteness all around.

The sheets, my PPE, my mask, the floor, the ceiling, her pillow, her hair.

All white.

I walked into her space behind the curtain and introduced myself from behind my clipboard.

I smiled wryly.

My colleague did too.

She couldn't see my heart underneath all the plastic I was wearing.

If she could, she would have seen it breaking for her.

'Good morning, Jane. My name is Natasha and this is my

colleague, Steph. We're here to see how you're going today.'

Jane stared at us deadpan.

Steph looked at me as if I was to provide the next, most sensible step.

I glanced over to Jane's bedside table. There was a cup of tea with the tea bag still inside the cup. It could have been there for hours. I peered inside the cup.

Floaties.

Steph's eyes crinkled kindly at our patient. I tipped the tea down the sink and proceeded to scrub my hand with a bit of soap from the large antibacterial tubs that hang so carefully beside every hospital sink. While singing the tune of 'Happy Birthday' (the recommended length of time to wash your hands in accordance with hand hygiene measures) and vigorously scrubbing every crevice of my hands, I probably had a thousand thoughts in the space of thirty seconds.

She honestly cannot speak functionally to me, right now.

The stroke took out her ability to verbalise.

We're going to have to think really fast here.

We've come to do language therapy.

Does she have a family?

Are they coming?

Surely someone could have made her a fresh tea?

Lucky that her swallowing has been assessed and she is able to drink tea. Depending on the location of the stroke, she may not have been able to consume her tea-incrusted floaties anyway.

Ew, that's gross.

I feel for her.

I have to do better for her.
This is hard.
Should I tell my supervisor?
Nope, I'm about a week out from finishing my clinical degree, I'm supposed to have this by now.
Okay, I've got this.
Well, we've got this.
Should I signal to Steph a 'we've got this' face?
Practise the skill of non-verbal communication?
We're supposed to be highly trained 'experts' at this by now
…Right, on with it.
… Happy Birthday to you.

I reached over and screeched the tap shut. I took a breath. Looked up and saw my face in the mirror.

My eyes met me back.

I had 'got this'.

Steph stepped back and I jumped into the role I knew too well. I was going to take the reins on this one.

'Kids?' I said, knowing Jane was able to understand more than she could say at that moment, so long as I spoke clearly and to the point.

I took a guess. Jane looked like she could have three kids aged somewhere between twenty-five and thirty-five.

She nodded, laboured and slow. Her eyes lit up at the thought of her children.

'That's lovely,' I replied. 'Jane, I noticed your tea was cold! I'm happy to make you another? We can check your swallowing too?'

I gestured 'swallowing' and pointed to my throat.

Jane shook her head.

Then, silence.

'Pink,' Jane croaked effortfully.

Pink.

Pink, what on Earth could that mean?

I felt the pressure rise in my chest. I so desperately wanted to understand what she was referring to.

So that she could feel some level of pre-stroke normal.

What I would have given in that moment to understand … I began racking my mind for anything I could hold on to, semantically related to pink.

I started, carefully: 'Flowers?'

Jane shook her head slowly.

Maybe it was lemonade? Something to replace her floaties tea with … no, that sounded too stupid to verbalise.

'The clouds … they are gorgeous,' I said, alluding to the wispy shapes moving in the afternoon sky. It was a stunner of a day outside the bars of the hospital room window.

Jane dropped her head, defeat all over her face.

'Pink?' I clarified, as if I had misheard it, knowing perfectly well that I hadn't.

I exchanged looks with Steph. She shrugged, subtle enough not to offend Jane.

Then, it landed.

'The singer?'

A smile crept over her face. Not symmetrical yet. Recovery is hard with stroke. It is literally written all over the face.

I gestured singing into a microphone. A slight nod of recognition from Jane was enough to keep me going.

In that moment, I realised why I had expended so much of my teenage energy into singing lessons and band practice, even though I was well aware at the time that my name was never going to be in stage lights.

For this.

I took a breath, set up my diaphragm and began to hum a melody to one of Pink's songs. I couldn't spend much time deciding which one, no time for that. Jane was helplessly waiting.

I finished my few lines of a rendition and waited.

Steph gave the eyes of encouragement, so I went on.

'Jane, do you like Pink? She's great, hey?'

And then, one of the most poignant moments of my clinical career occurred in front of my eyes, before I ever even had a chance to experience anything further.

'*Wait a second, we're not broken, just bent and we can learn to love again …*' Jane *sang* the words.

The words on her mind.

The words she could muster from her left-side brain and transmute over to the right. She channelled them into her vocal folds. She attempted with great might to hit the notes in the right key.

She waited for me to continue our duet.

Steph was the most gracious audience member in our space. She walked over to Jane, amazed, and propped up her pillows.

If you ever want to marvel at the thought of universal

balance, you need to look no further than watching a beautiful, bent brain attempt to repair itself.

The left and right brains exist within the realm of their own Divine Dance. Where one area lacks, the other attempts to repair. It is a true partnership—cohesive and pure. No matter how long I've been practising or what clinical case walks through the door, I am always amazed anew. It's as if I am witnessing the marvel that is the human brain every single time.

Nothing sets off that reaction more than when engaging a client in a speech-language therapy session post left-side stroke. It is not uncommon to see a patient battling either some level of aphasia (language impairment), as most of our human population experience the language centre of their brain in the left hemisphere. Aphasia can manifest either receptively, impacting your ability to understand the messages of language; expressively, attacking your ability to express a linguistic message; or globally, whereby both receptive and expressive language is impacted.

In the realm of communication, the right brain is responsible for our pragmatic communication function, our social reasoning, and our emotive aspects of communication. When a singer taps into the raw emotion that comes with a vocal performance, the right brain is responsible for bringing the audience those all-too-visceral goosebumps.

One of the most inspiring kids I've ever met had her entire life flipped upside down when a paediatric stroke overcame her body and targeted her right brain. My little friend, Ave, was a gifted dancer. Her face lit up a stage and her movements were fluid and graceful. A great honour of mine has been being on Ave's rehab team. Ave was literally learning, all over again, how to find her fluidity. The stroke meant that everything became rigid—from her walking to making friendships.

Ave's superpowers are her smile and her sass. Her superstar quality is innate. While her brain was healing, she healed others with her inspiration and she will continue to do so for the rest of her life.

Ave's parents and I have had many a conversation around what life will look like for Ave as she enters adulthood. While, again, that mystical crystal ball has never shown up with its long-awaited reveal, we know for sure that adversity bore a strength in this beautiful girl that can only continue to inspire anyone who crosses her path. That level of inspirational impact transcends our understanding of what's *right* and *fair* in this world, and forces us to go beyond the immediate experience and come full circle with the understanding of what is, ultimately, the depth of human strength.

In addition to aphasia, the patient may be presenting with some form of motor speech disorder, which implicates the verbal component of communication. Jane's aphasia was largely expressive. At the time of seeing her, she was barely able to retrieve and verbalise one single word at a time. Generally speaking, words of high interest and importance are likely to be the most accessible. The brain has a somewhat efficient way of sorting this stuff out. This phenomenon is observed when intensive therapy is conducted appropriately and in a timely fashion, however, each case is independent and seeing one stroke definitely *does not* mean you've 'seen it all'.

Neurologically, Jane's brain was demonstrating the epitome of neuroplasticity—the potential for the brain to rewire itself after some kind of trauma or adverse event. It is almost as though, as humans, we carry with us an in-built management system. A natural 'backup' for when life gives us a hiccup.

As we explored in Chapter 2, the drive towards homeostasis is a biologically motivated program seeking balance. In the case of Jane's brain, a very specific compensatory event was occurring between her left and right hemispheres. Our brains also contain the corpus callosum, a large mass of nerve fibres—the major 'highway system' of the brain, if you will—that when intact, enables the left and the right brain to communicate. Her neural pathways had registered that her language and speech centres were suboptimal and so her right brain stepped up to 'assist'.

Jane's right brain wanted to communicate her message.

Her inner voice was her silent strength.

She mustered all the energy in her left brain to conjure up the word 'pink'. And while, in this example, the triumph of that therapy session was dependent on me and Steph playing detective, the power of connection was the driving force behind a very successful intervention pathway for Jane. We took the motivation of the right brain and rehabbed, very carefully, commonplace words and those of meaning one at a time, through the function of singing and music.

Sometimes I wonder if music artists know the true power of their melodies.

I bow down to the power of the human voice and our fascination with making music our safe space.

Sound is our healer. It vibrates in and amongst our cells and nurses us back to our health.

We make sound so we can oscillate in perfect harmony with nature.

I unpack this idea clinically and personally with my Travelling Partner and colleague, Kirsty, on a regular basis. It helps us to show up for our clients—even on days where we are energetically spent and at the mercy of our role.

As we've said many times before on the matter: hold the space and the rest will fall into place.

Your mess is your message

'Your mess is your message' is yet another phrase that continues to shape my world view, although I have no idea where I first heard it. It just felt imperative though, so it is something that comes in and out of my awareness when I need it most.

We all have a desire to communicate. It is also a human right.

Clinically, I do seem to attract the clients with a complex background. As you can appreciate from Travelling Partners, this doesn't surprise or necessarily 'throw' me—I am fully accepting of my role and place in this world. When you are studying any discipline in the space of medicine or allied health, a majority of your degree is tailored to specific 'patient populations' or areas of practice. In running my own business that has been largely successful on a word-of-mouth basis, much of my patient population is paediatric and, in particular, centred on one very fascinating neurological condition; a condition that has taught me more about my own voice than any study or hours of vocal coaching ever have.

The autism spectrum is absolutely beautiful in all its mystery. It is a mind-boggling space to navigate and extremely rewarding to work in.

Over the years spent in my clinic room, no other condition has continued to challenge me personally and professionally like autism has.

After a stint working in one of Sydney's busiest hospitals, I decided it was time to go out there on my own and open a private practice full time. I could not wait.

First appointment
9:00 am on day one of full-time private practice.

'I don't know if I'm cut out to handle this.' She cried silently in the corner. The silence of her tears fell in sync with the silence of the space. She looked over and watched her son intently. He was happily playing with the trucks I had out on the floor. Spinning the wheels and observing in real time the phenomenon of rotational inertia ...

Spinning and turning. Repetitive movement. So calming for this little friend of mine.

His mother stared in utter bewilderment, glancing her son up and down, watching every subtle shift in his movements. Trying desperately to process the reality of his unknown inner world.

'I just don't understand. Why can't anyone tell me if I will ever hear his voice? I want to know what he is thinking. I just want to connect.'

I encouraged the emotional dust in the room to settle.

I encouraged the silence.

'We don't know.'

It is always the hardest answer to give.

'All we can do is work our hardest and provide as many opportunities to verbalise as we can. We'll navigate it as we go, as he gets older … as his needs change, as his motivations shift …'

She nodded in recognition as she sniffed away her tears.

'Thank you.'

I could tell it was not the answer she would have preferred, but it would suffice—for today.

Moments moved on.

My little friend in the corner was still spinning the wheels on the truck next to him. I figured the red one must be his favourite. He kept coming back to it.

The silence was broken by the sound of a hum. My little friend breathed out a beautiful tune from his vocal folds.

'See that, do you think that'll turn into words? Like, perhaps not today or tomorrow … but surely, eventually?'

'It is a wonderful sound, isn't it? His voice …' I smiled gently. I let her receive my smile so that she could take in the next thought, sincerely. '… his voice is there. Whether he will hold a conversation with us remains to be seen, but it is our job as his number-one supporters to help facilitate his messages so that he can communicate them with his world. There are many things we can try that are both verbal and non-verbal. We are guided by him. He will show us how he prefers to communicate. We just need to pay attention.'

She continued to cry quietly, but this time, she smiled back.

'Okay, thank you. I'm glad we're here.'

'I'm glad you are too.'

I sat down next to my little friend and began to play with a truck nearby. I joined in with his humming. At first, my presence did not engage him, but after a few minutes, I got the side-eye glance—not uncommon in the clinic space.

I knew we were going to be friends.

Expression, particularly verbal, is often the most compromised clinical aspect of non-verbal ASD (formally autism spectrum disorder). Often, and depending on the integrity of adjacent neural pathways, there are sensory factors at play that either facilitate or inhibit one's communicative capacity. As you can imagine, our practice rooms are filled with a wild scale of all-encompassing human emotion. In a single therapy session alone, we can sometimes experience hysterical laughter, uncontrollable tears and astronomical levels of frustration all within a space of half an hour. The emotional process is touched by everyone in that therapy space—the client, their family and their managing therapist. It really is a space for deep processing and incredible learning.

The one certainty I have to share with my beautiful case load of clients is this—your 'mess', the thing that makes you feel tangled and unsure, is often your greatest strength.

Your message, your truth.

The thing that the world needs to learn from you.

The rest of the Universe is relying on you to learn so that you can teach.

Pioneer change.

Advocate for difference.

Correct imbalances.

Ultimately, your mess gives the world its authentic *voice*—even when the voice is momentarily silent.

Stillness speaks volumes.

Stillness settles the heart and invites us back—

To balance.

Life or death?

Two weeks into lockdown, 2020

I was nauseated. Perpetually.

I was two days into knowing why. It hadn't fully landed though.

The double line had appeared. The life-confirming line.

The ultimate lifeline.

Vincent and I were over-the-moon delighted and equally processing *all of the things*.

Most pressing of all—raising a child.

In a pandemic. One without an end date.

Well, this was unprecedented territory, to say the least.

We came to the conclusion that we were going to be sharing our news with our special ones over Zoom or FaceTime.

Sign of the times, right?

The decision was simple—I needed to out the news to someone. I figured it couldn't be family because it wouldn't be fair: how was I supposed to pick who got Zoom privilege first? With COVID came new conventions.

So naturally, I went to the safe space. We were used to creating it together by now.

As I went to dial Mitch's number, the little voice spoke to me. So clearly.

In that moment, I prayed she wasn't right. Just this one time.

It was the same voice that hit me right in the centre of my chest and strangled my vocal folds the second I realised I was being told that Dylan had hit a tree all those years ago—the intuitive nudge that bad news was about to land.

I wasn't sure if it was Baby or the thought that made me feel more nauseous.

I knew he was awaiting some news too but figured that surely news of that magnitude couldn't be dealt on the same day. *Surely*.

I scrolled my phone under 'Recent'. I didn't need to scroll far. Lockdown meant that chatting daily was as commonplace as fighting for toilet paper in Woolies.

We skipped hellos and any forms of politeness markers.

This was likely conversation number three that day anyway.

'... I have news.'

'Like, news that's different from a few hours ago?' His tone was serious.

'Yes, like, very different ...' I started.

I was trying to manage my phone and my headset while hanging the clothes on the line. Lockdown was good for catching up on copious amounts of laundry. I chose a peg that was rusting at the bottom of the barrel. It snapped. I bent down to pick it up. Then stood up too quickly.

Ugh, the nausea.

I turned my attention back to the conversation.

Now nervous, and nauseated.

'Me too, you first.'

I thought I knew where it was going ...

I blurted, 'I am with child. There is a human alien growing in my womb space.'

The line crackled. Shock and then the most poignant congratulations I've ever received.

I knew it was my turn.

'It's palliative, isn't it?'

Silence.

Then, the most poignant apology I've ever given.

'I'm so sorry.'

While most people were fretting over their pantry supply levels and whether or not they had enough hand sanitiser to go into battle, Mitch had a very real battle on his hands. He and his mother were sole carers for his very sick but otherwise very sprightly brother. Now, as I was seemingly hearing, with months to live.

The nausea was definitely not Baby this time.

We stayed on the line.

Just in that space. The space we had created in the car five years earlier, the day he came out to me.

'You are so loved,' I almost whispered down the phone.

'I know, so are you. And so is this baby and Dalton,' he finished quickly.

'Absolutely. I got you.'

'Always.'

'Life, hey?'

'Yep. Life.'

The manual

We aren't born with a manual. Especially when it comes to dealing with adversity. From a young age, we are shown that happiness is the ideal state.

Ask any child with a birthday coming up.

Dopamine, in the form of present opening, wearing stupid hats and sending out invites is mainstream and *normal*. And really, it is beautiful. It is teaching the young one to celebrate life. But that is also the greatest flaw in our childhood narrative.

How do you set someone up for the parts of life that are definitely less than celebratory?

Or dare we say *mundane*?

Or not the script we thought we were offered at the audition.

How do we teach our little ones that instant gratification is a slippery slope when we are all just getting our next hit from somewhere? Not everyone's drug of choice is illicit. Some of us just need a late-night scroll to hit all the nerves in 'all the right places'.

And in doing that, we are winding up our nervous systems. We then go on a wild goose chase to *unlearn* behaviour. We enrol in courses, go to therapy, try all the things …

And then no one ever tells you to be patient with yourself either. That once you've started that quest for growth and healing, it may take years to have the undoing, done.

And yet another fallacy hits home. Even the wellness industry, mostly unintentionally, sets us up to want *instant gratification with our healing.*

Life simply does not work like that.

Come home to yourself instead. That's all the adversity manual need say.

Healing will likely go for the course of your life. As the Universe brings in the lessons for you, you will be shown the majesty in the madness.

That is the human condition.

That is a universal condition. The relentless desire for homeostasis. Inward and outward.

The more readily we are willing to accept this and hold space for this reality too, the deeper our healing goes.

The soul knows nourishment when all sides are looked at.

Loved. Appreciated.

Let's not make the shadow the black-sheep child.

The shadow holds equal brilliance.
We have just been led to believe that it doesn't.
This too will *always* pass.

Listening

I had one of my truest inner-child healing sessions with my sister about four months after I got married. We weren't living together anymore for obvious reasons. It was not a reiki session or perfectly timed meditation. I wasn't even seeking 'healing' at the point that the lesson landed.

My sister Nat is my mirror. She's two years younger than me, and her reflection has always bounced off mine. Being so close in age, we often took turns on life's milestones, until we got older and our life stages began to get foggy. When we were younger, there were clear division points. The end of primary school for her, the beginning of high school for me. The end of high school for her, the beginning of university for me. We did that dance well until life got messy and our twenties became just that, our *twenties.*

Through teenage depression, OCD and my generally messed-up psyche, Nat was always my sounding board. Never uttering a word, just lending her shoulder at silly hours of the morning. Our dynamic was never challenged. I never asked her permission, though. I just assumed she subscribed to it, just the way I pitched it to her, before she was even born.

I spoke, she listened. That was the deal.

Nat and I attended a kids' yoga course together for one

month within the first year of clinically working together. Another thing she and I did well was blur our personal and professional lines. We started our professional careers in the same workplace. We still work together.

On the way back from the course, we were half an hour deep into a discussion about how to teach the chakra system to little ones. We love a good niche conversation.

We were running a therapeutic wellbeing group at a prestigious school in Sydney's east at the time. These kids were begging for a breath and often leading lives less than childlike. Carving out this program was a challenge on a few fronts, to say the least.

'I feel I could take the lead on the throat chakra chat,' I began after a few back and forths with problem solving.

'Why would you say that?' Nat questioned. I was caught off guard. She has a way of being very direct with her communication—most of the time.

'... Well, what else do I do for a living? I've got tons of ideas around vocal chants and fun verbal games to play.'

Nat's face fell. She went deep into a thought process that felt unnatural against the momentum of conversation up to that point.

'... I'm sorry, I'm taking it,' she said. 'Of the two of us, I can teach a thing or two about *listening*. You are *still* learning that lesson. Sure, verbalising and using your voice is therapeutic and important, but there is more magic in the silence. If we're teaching kids to balance their throat chakra, how about teaching them to listen to themselves? In silence? ... You don't need to fill every space, Tash.'

I turned to her, mouth open, ready to speak back; my argument predetermined in my head.

Her eyes instructed me otherwise. For one of the first times in my life, closing my mouth said more than enough.

'How are you still learning *that*!' she screeched. Pent-up, fed-up anger coated her words.

She was triggered, I was triggered.

We continued to drive for the next hour.

In silence.

The lesson

We are here to learn to speak our truth. Our truth will almost always be tied up in navigating some form of adversity.

Adversity often confronts us with the life/death equation and/or a less-than-ideal health event.

But sometimes it's a car-ride conversation that undoes all you've ever known about yourself and forces you to take a hard look at how you've been showing up.

Human beings, susceptible to pain.

Adaptable to change.

Questions for your soul work

1
How has adversity forced perspective onto you?

———•———

2
What has your shadow taught you about balance?

———•———

3
What is true for you today that might not be if it weren't for adversity?

———•———

4
How do you navigate adversity? Do your practices need to change?

———•———

5
What 'mess' has life dished up for you that you can transmute into messages?

CHAPTER 8

Observable Reality

The Lesson: A cellular inhale is a collective exhale.

Space to breathe

I sat, socially distanced and masked amongst my colleagues.

That time of the year had rolled around again and we were seated in your gold-standard CPR/first-aid training. This one felt different though.

The trainer and I had argued over which nut mylk tasted better in our morning coffee and already accurately guessed each other's star sign, so I knew that on some level, this was going to be slightly more bearable than your run-of-the-mill, checkbox training.

'Cut, deep wound, bleeding relentlessly and likely to become infected … describe your bandaging technique,' Luke rattled off. He was eager with his teaching style and one of those 'I'll fire a question at you off guard' types. I couldn't afford to space out today.

'Two finger spaces between the skin and the bandage,' echoed my colleague Jen, verbatim.

'Why?' pressed Luke to the group, but specifically striking eye contact with me. My turn to have a go.

'To create space,' I started, sure of myself but leaving room for correction.

'For what?' he harped on with momentum.

'For the wound.'

'To do … what? …'

This guy was an ellipsis personified.

'For the wound to create swelling as it 'does its thing'.'

'Yes. Yes—that right there is what I'm talking about, folks. To halt the blood flow from a wound, we need to provide adequate wrapping but allow space for the bleed … we must also strike the balance to give way for the swelling … the swelling, the 'bigness' around the wound kickstarts the healing process.'

As soon as he finished speaking, I decided that I loved that our bodies do that. I parked that in the short-term memory bank and made a mental note to jot down the idea after the course.

An hour or so later, we were thrust into revision on choking and anaphylaxis.

Luke was again in his prime teaching element.

'Our bodies, when unconscious, will naturally seek the ground. We do this involuntarily when we faint. Our bodies crave the ground. Gravity takes over as we seek the safety of shutdown.'

I knew I was supposed to be making notes for our theory quiz that was likely going to be thrust upon us at the end of the day, but my mind went elsewhere quickly.

I was thinking about how the manuscript for the very book you are reading would be due in less than a month. And how, at the end of it all, humans are looking for two things in particular at any one time.

Space and grounding.

Whether it be oedema swelling into effect after an invasive wound, or years of the rollercoaster ride after major trauma, or fainting to reset the nervous system after a choking event, or keeping sane during a global pandemic—

We simply need space.

Emotional resonance needs an echo chamber, beyond the walls of the heart.

We look to draw a parallel with the ground.

We crave Mother Earth.

We crave her water, her shelter, her roots and her sunshine.

We ground with her and for her.

Our reality and all that can possibly be observed, from the cellular to the celestial, is attempting to achieve the 'sweet spot'.

And when we reach that place, we look for our breath.

Breath in the 2020s feels different so far.

Our inhales and our exhales lack depth.

Yet, we've never before needed the space to *breathe* as we do now.

Literally—behind the mask and the locked door of our neighbour's house.

Pneuma is the Universal code for balance.

One man's search for breath even started a well-overdue global movement.

'I can't breathe'—the last words on his breath.

Even with life slowed down to the point of a looping groundhog day, we still can't quite seem to catch our breath.

Our perception of space is lacking.

When there is no such balance

In the world we currently live in—with a virus causing a ruckus, mass protests against almost anything you could think of, and the internet being, well *the internet*—we are, ironically, more than ever, toxically divided.

It seems as if Universe is momentarily dealing with the exact opposite of what this title is proclaiming to be—

The Unbalanced Theory.

Our observable reality has left much to be desired.

As we are nearing the end of this exploration together, I feel pulled to say this: I feel as though you could have been browsing your favourite online bookshop, or perhaps you were running your fingers along the spines of titles in the quaint bookstore down the road (or perhaps not, because lockdown), and were feeling a little misguided. You landed on the title *The Balance Theory*, saw the author was a coach, and likely picked up this book in the hope that I'd have a sure-fire answer to the elusive, never-seem-to-be-achieving 'work/life balance' trap that we all have succumbed to at one point or other.

Well, here is my official apology that this book was definitely not *that* book.

It almost seems like a book with the title *The Balance Theory* should allude to the idea at some point, so I'll take this opportunity to share my thoughts on this one now that the work/life balance trap is truly part of our observable reality.

There is no such thing.

Really, there isn't.

After seven chapters of deep-dive and a deliberate exposé on the Universe doing its thing to keep us reminded of the sanctity of life itself, balance in the work/life equation does not have a place. Various coaching circles will speak to the idea of 'work/life' integration and the like, but I challenge this at its very core.

Why don't we collectively call it anything other than 'work/life'? Why do we prop the word 'work' against the rest of our lives? When did we permit 'work' to have fifty per cent of that equation against all the things that encompass our lives in total? How have we not picked that up over the course of history until ... *now*?

Something's got to give. It does not matter how well rounded you are, how many courses you've taken, what tricks of the trade you've tried and adapted.

The search for balance is nothing but a search—but that in and of itself is the Universal goal.

That experience is more than enough.

The journey towards balance is more earnest than the destination. In chasing the elusive concept of balance in day-to-day life, the real nugget is in the exploration of *self-awareness*.

That is:

- Becoming self-aware of *where* your energy is channelled and who in your life receives that energy; who you choose to devote your time, money and resources to
- Becoming self-aware of the stories you've had drummed into you and what you continue to keep telling yourself as a result

- Becoming self-aware of the beliefs that live somewhere in the back of your head and that like to come out to bite at the most inconvenient moments

Self-awareness puts the ego to rest when required, although can stir it up accordingly when it needs to be in the arena to serve.

Fully functioning self-awareness is kind, compassionate and self-loving. It is mother energy making a home-cooked meal on Sunday afternoon.

I'll throw in this realisation. During my years studying coaching, I made a pact with myself that I would never again *feel* as though I was dictated by the material construct of time. I decided that time was going to work for me, rather than against me.

No, I did not somehow manifest an extra few hours of the day.

I did not make a deal with the calendar lords and request another day in the week.

I stopped bargaining with whoever is in charge of the Time Flies Committee.

Instead, I had a good hard look at my schedules, my diaries (personal and professional) and my goals and did absolutely nothing physical.

I decided to decide differently.

I chose to feel into my emotional field to guide my direction toward balance. I began to use my internal world to drive my external reality.

For someone with recovering type A personality traits,

this was effortful and almost *forced* at the beginning. But some short time after my ninety-day mental experiment, the subconscious shifts started to play out in real time. Everything became a matter of priority. I put my OCD to work in a specific and beneficial way. My therapist was always quick to remind me that for every supposed 'weakness' of mental illness, there was a strength. While I could never really see that at the time of diagnosis, it was amounting to this.

An assiduous teaching.

That word, assiduous. One of my favourite meditations uses that exact word and suggests that assiduous life lessons, when moved through in light of healing, have the power to *enhance your immunity.*

Literally strengthen your immune response.

The capacity to shift your observable reality.

As an extension of being impeccable with your energy—be impeccable with where energy is being directed. It can look as simple as writing a list of all the things taking up space in your mind and carefully examining the place of and capacity for each one. It can look like a five-minute morning sit with a coffee and mentally gearing up for the day before anyone or anything else takes your energy.

You gatekeep your own gateway. Never allow anyone to take that power away from you.

I observed my reality and chose to act, think, walk and talk in favour of my goals. I allowed my ego a healthy and measured dose of the limelight as I carefully performed this life audit over eighteen months, so that I could dissolve her.

There were three words that stuck out at the core of this process as I set out to consciously create my reality: *help*, *heal* and *hinder*.

The three Hs

Every thought we allow to penetrate and linger in our minds has the power to either *hinder*, *help* or *heal* our reality.

Life's three Hs.

While most of our daily thoughts are automated and on subconscious loop, as we've previously come to know, the choice is in the capacity to reconstruct our mental faculties to work for us by calling out the hindrance, adjusting the script to something helpful and ultimately use that wisdom to heal our immediate experience of what's 'real'.

If there was ever a time to dissect this process, it would be now. At the time of writing this chapter, the date is 7 April 2020.

The context, being an Australian this year is such: We've experienced a country on fire, followed by floods that washed out the debris—both literally and figuratively—and, along with the rest of the world, a virus that holds a destructive power like never before in recent history.

I'm currently curled up on my couch on an afternoon tea break between seeing clients via telehealth.

Adapted, to say the least.

At the beginning of a new year (every year since Dylan's passing), I ask myself the following question: *What do I not know now that I'd be shocked to know by 31 December of this year?*

At the end of 2019, I asked myself that very question and even chuckled in surrender. The response to that question feels like it's getting more ridiculous as the years have rolled on. I've quite enjoyed the amusement that has come with observing rapid changes over the past five years particularly, when I reflect on my responses.

Wrapping Christmas presents at the end of 2019, I remember feeling intuitively that the energy was going to be huge, but I couldn't quite put my finger on what exactly I was picking up on. I just knew it was going to be life changing.

And it felt collective.

End of March, 2020

Well, energy never lies, because it's safe to say, a few things have definitely changed:

a.   The entire world is on bed rest indefinitely.

b.   The entire world is experiencing the raw essence of fear and the lessons are pouring in fast and hard. There appears to be 'manuals for getting through' on every media channel known to man and yet nobody has a clue how to navigate this.

c.   The entire world is being forced into alignment at lightning speed.

Never has there been a call to balance like there is today.

The call has been fierce and unabated.

As I munch on my banana bread (that I had time to make by hand this week), I am reminded, so overtly, of the call to rest. In particular, rest being just as if not more important than the *work*. I also have no idea what's around the corner for my business or our family planning, or whether or not I'll have toilet paper tomorrow and I can honestly say, I've also never had more trust in surrendering to the divine plan as I do today.

With blind faith comes a blind sense of knowing.

And with that knowing, the veils are off. If we drop the resistance bands, we will see that all the Universe ever did was give—and give unapologetically this time.

The memes circulating cyberspace at the moment have been nothing short of a saving grace, because the current situation feels so far-fetched that you have to laugh to avoid constant crying.

Ultimately, where you were at the time that COVID-19 stopped you in your tracks was where you were always meant to be. Your lessons, gifted in one very uncertain capsule of time.

For some, discomfort.

Others, bliss—an excuse to slow down while making ends meet from the comfort of the couch.

Then there were those who well and truly experienced loss of Self overnight to the point of questioning, *Who am I when I'm forced into isolation?*

Whichever side of the fence you sit on when it comes to the vaccination debate is irrelevant. COVID-19 has manifested as more than a virus. It is an equaliser. It does not discriminate. It is in our vortex beyond its physical effects. It is here to get us to 'pull our heads in' on a mass scale.

In the first lockdown, I sat to channel the collective. I shared it with my Instagram community, and today, eighteen months into the pandemic, it remains as true as it did that day:

> Love each other. Turn to each other (emotionally and mentally). The irony of social distancing is to touch base with what's actually real.
>
> Human connection.
>
> Compassion.
>
> Empathy.
>
> This is a warning to use technology wisely.
>
> Use it kindly.
>
> Use it to let go of fear.

This virus is just visiting, like many other phenomena on the planet.

It's threatening our observable existence to bring in a new one.

To reteach our collective consciousness what it is to truly connect with one another.

It's forcing us home.

Home in our hearts.

Home in our minds.

Home on this earth.

Connect first to yourself and then send love to Other.

Nothing can cancel that.

Radical expression

Interestingly, I let go of this chapter completely at the time of writing it. The very first weekend of New South Wales lockdown in April 2020 was the time I learned of my special starseed planting his way into existence.

It was also the weekend of my fateful phone call to Mitch and you know now how that went.

The rest of the year was a massive pivot: grieving the death of my beloved Travelling Partner, Sandra (you'll meet her in Chapter 9); holding space for Mitch as his brother took flight from this lifetime; preparing for my baby; completely moving my clinical practice online; and of course, facing the pandemic, pregnant.

2020 was relentless with the lessons for sure.

August 2021

Cut to New South Wales lockdown 2.0. My eight-month-old son, Alfie, smiling so innocently as he downed his quinoa and beetroot lunch. Life inside our four walls was wholesome. The rest of the world had different ideas. The sun infiltrated the window and warmed me so comfortably across the face. A reminder that any other given year, we would probably have taken a drive down the coast on a day like today.

We would not have wasted that precious sunshine.

But we had no choice today.

We were in the thick of it.

Again.

I'd just spoken to my family, scared all around Victoria—from Mildura to Melbourne—experiencing lockdown number 'can't keep up'.

There was a heaviness that was undeniable.

At that time, a year and a half post the first lockdown, I had coined a new term—*Pivot Fatigue*. Pivot Fatigue, as I had discussed with Kirsty earlier in the week, is exactly what it implies—the tiredness that comes with having to adapt, again, after finally getting used to a new way of living, devising a new routine and/or scratching for some form of 'normal' in a completely unprecedented set of circumstances.

Pivot Fatigue is the mantra for pandemic life for sure.

This day, Pivot Fatigue was at an all-time high. Just plain tired from having to make quick changes with total uncertainty, when it goes against all intuitive urges in your nervous system.

I checked my phone, consciously. Mindless 'doomscrolling', as Vincent calls it, was something I was specifically attempting not to make a habit of this time around. But it was bloody difficult—there was so much noise. From ridiculous memes about the state of our government to anti-vax protest stories, the ruckus found its way into the peace of my family home through every media outlet, from mainstream to social and even niche podcasts of choice.

This particular day, I'd opened up a group chat between my girlfriends. It's so lovely to have a collective soapbox when you feel the need to be frustrated with the world but aren't prepared to cop the wrath of opinions on a public scale.

Group chats were the new secret societies, I figured.

I dragged my finger down the chat, as you do when you haven't opened it for a few hours, and had missed copious amounts of memes and photos from the Sunday morning catch-up. I could tell, straight away, my beautiful friend Mel was pissed today. And full credit to her, she was entitled to it. She'd had her fair share of needing to 'grin and bear it' for this lifetime. Losing her incredible mother when we were fourteen should have been enough, but Mel has definitely seen a lump of hardships beyond that time too. She is the purest form of a Travelling Partner for me; there is not a single life lesson that has come to fruition for me that did not somehow involve Mel.

We were used to nutting out our existentialism together. Today was no different.

Her rant was warranted and necessary. Enraged at the state of the division at all levels —between leaders, the community, family and friends. An absolutely unfathomable situation for a Pisces Moon.

There was no consoling today. That was not what Mel was after. She just needed to be heard.

*The obsession with numbers, with cases is just overwhelming. I can stay home, I can 'do my part' but it just seems pointless on a mental level. If we blow it out and look over it, on a global scale, what the f*ck are we doing?!*

We left space for it to land because really, she was right.

Humans have a fantastic way of completely missing the point.

In trying so desperately to make a point, we miss another.

There, in a peak of lockdown and extreme stay-at-home orders, we aired our dirty laundry and shared just how dirty we were with the rest of the world, alone.

Together.

I sat in meditation that afternoon, jumped eagerly into my perspex box and locked the door. I even made the box suffocatingly smaller than usual so that I could only see and hear myself amongst the noise. I lay down in the fetal position, my knees pushed up against the glass, my head touching one end and my feet the other. And I sank into a hypnotic memory of mine.

I was immediately taken back to the conversation I had had with Lucy over a cup of tea, all those years ago when I first voiced The Balance Theory out loud. My own voice ran rapid in my mind but I was so aware that the voice behind that voice was coming from somewhere else:

> Universe delivers inscrutable tragedy so we can see the truth. Natural disasters, pandemics, mass death, terrorism, racism ... all the 'isms' ... these phenomena are not supposed to unite you because of pain. They are supposed to call you to your humanity ... a collective uplifting.
>
> When humans haven't been listening, Universe has no choice but to 'send' a confrontational wake-up call. Should there be more division when the call is heralded, then Universe will show up again to reteach the very same thing, in a different costume.
>
> This is what it is to be human. The suffering is the teacher; it comes from you, for you. The pain is the collective imprint. It's asking you to look behind you and pick up your fellow person. Help each other, to heal each other. That's the

only rule in the book. Universe will hinder in order to heal. Once that's figured out, you'll be able to rise.

That afternoon, we came to this.

Radical acceptance of what is.

But it comes with a proviso.

In the short term, and for the sake of your own mental health, radically accept that the outside world is exactly that—outside of you.

In the long term and for the betterment of humanity and all the generations to come, practise *radical expression*.

It is your duty as a global community member to express the highest version of yourself, in whatever modality you wish to do that.

The intention will always shine through the cause. Start in your immediate community and build momentum over time.

Find your thing and nail its highest expression—

Start a composting company for sustainability.

Hug your dog a little tighter and fight for animal rights.

Work on your craft and release the song that will be sung for years to come.

Write the game-changing book.

Start a forum for honest conversations.

Donate for the sake of your Afghan sisters and call out injustice.

Wear your rainbow with pride.

Expression is what moves the needle in this world.

It is the vehicle for the correction of imbalances.

Humanity is the problem and the solution.

The lesson

We've said it before and it is so powerful, it needs to be restated: Universe never promised fairness. But it did promise truths.

Exposing humanity is Universe's finest act.

Energy doesn't lie. Energetics are as concrete as science; you just need to know where to look for your evidence.

Human behaviour is your proof that we are learning, at an exponential rate, the importance of harmony in the quest for balance.

Humans cycle. We've never known how to draw a straight line.

Historically, we've hidden behind lines of militant soldiers. Precise, numb and ready to be wounded. But all wounds need space.

Curiosity invites us to step over the line.

We've pushed the pendulum so far that the collective comeback is on wrecking-ball level.

We are weapons of mass destruction in our own right.

This is our observable reality.

Questions for your soul work

1

What is the relationship between the outer world and your inner world right now?

2

How can you practise personal alignment despite external world events?

3

What are your biggest learnings from inner fear?

4

What are your biggest learnings from outer fear?

5

What does *radical acceptance* mean to you? Have you ever considered practising it and working backwards from that point?

6

What does *radical expression* look like for you?

7

The Universe is attempting to balance itself on a mass level. How does that statement feel for you?

8

Reflection Activity: Create space for reflection on COVID-19. List the lessons, the learnings, the frustrations and the 'aha moments'. Write a letter to yourself in fifty years' time to remind you of the strength that you fostered during such a turbulent global time. Set an intention for your reflection before going into the writing space. Stay curious with what comes up.

CHAPTER 9

Kismet Connection

The Lesson: Connection to Self, Other and the world is ultimately kismet. Balance is a divine Universal act.

Is it possible?

Is it possible that all we are is energy?
Energy passing through,
Ourselves.
Vessels of energy, cultivating energy.
Electric. Cosmic.
Somewhere in between?
But not limited in the way they teach us in chemistry class.
As it stands, we have positive ions.
Negative ions.
And thus far, it serves us well to know they both exist.
What if it were true that nothing was weighted either way?
Would we be free if we let go altogether?
As individuals.
As a race.
What if the Universe was trying to tell us to not give it any weight all along?
And that our mind is a filter; a barrier which forces weight—
Perspective isn't really real at all.

What if together,
We were able to transcend?
We would arrive, collectively, at a place where nothing was weighted anymore ...

Imagine a ball of pure white light.
The essence of Life itself.
Now imagine it passes through a tunnel, made from itself.
The tunnel is perfectly circular.
Signifying there is no beginning and no end.
There is just existence.
Now, you.
In human form.
You are constantly creating this tunnel with your Spirit;
Your energy.
But your view is from the Top.
In this moment, you are now Everything.
Past, present, future, from this realm, from the next, across time and space.
Across all dimensions.
And the ball of light travels through the tunnel.
The way ahead is clear.
There are no obstacles for this energy consumption as it takes place.
No positive ions.
No negative ones either.
Clarity only.
It goes beyond the science we were taught in class.

We have arrived on the spiritual plane Now.
A light, conscious Space.
Travelling.
As the Energy rolls through with ease, grace, it begins to manifest into two.
And two becomes three. And three becomes twenty and twenty, a hundred.
A hundred, a thousand, ten thousand and more.
And eventually, a million.
A billion, even.
Exponential Energy now.
And all the Travelling Partners to exist on this planet share the space in the tunnel.
The sacred energy field they all call home.
There is comfort,
There is beauty;
Intrinsically linked.
It's human and so much more.
It's the way we connect.
It's why we connect.
Because all the Universe wants at this moment is Balance.
And all it's ever tried to tell us
Is that that's okay.
Not positive, not negative.
Just is.

What if I told you that your mind was the tunnel?
Your capacity to experience this life on Earth only exists

within the domain of mind.
You'd have the whole world as a potential Travelling Partner.
You create your own reality.
Such gorgeous potential in this pure happiness.
So, while the Universe wants balance, and the energy passes through you,
Your one job is to simply trust it.
The energy knows what it wants.
It never lies.
It knows its destination.
Let your mind be the guiding tunnel in this life.
For yourself and all sentient beings who are stabilising the energy on either side of you.
In celebration of consciousness itself—
You.

Calculated safety

I am a 'numbers' person, but not in the way you would think. Tax time does my head in, as do the spreadsheets and graphs that come with it, but those who know me well have often echoed back to me that I enjoy quantifying things. I'd never really even noticed this about myself until I was away with Alex. My beautiful friend and I were overstimulated and exhausted coming off the back of a twenty-two-hour haul from Sydney to New York City. We headed straight for Times Square.

Keen to explore, we zipped from Newark Airport through

highways and tunnels until we landed, asleep with eyes wide open, in the heart of it all. The offensive yellow arches of the McDonald's sign kept us awake despite the insatiable desire to sleep.

Then, my overwhelmed mind in sensory overload started verbalising all the questions:

'Al, how many people do you think fit into this square?'

'How many people do you think are in the queue?'

'How many tourists do you think get to the Top of the Rock every day?'

'Tash,' she began gently, as she always does, 'you do realise you ask a lot of questions ... mostly about numbers.'

I cocked my head to the side and gave her the 'huh' eyes.

Then we laughed hysterically together, delirious from jet lag.

Al leaned her head on my shoulder as we looked up and took in the Victoria's Secret billboard featuring some soon-to-be-famous supermodel. In that space, amongst the hustle and bustle, the yellow blur of cabs whizzing around us, and the sound of a bunch of street kids' boom box pounding at a new level of bass for my eardrums, I had one of the most spiritual realisations of my life, courtesy of Al.

Numbers have always eased my anxiety.

They've always helped me to make sense of this madness when it tips over from 'manageable' to 'mayhem'.

Numbers are sacred, geometric and safe.

Numbers are the bridge between science and spirit; one of the few things on this planet that can't be denied.

The pattern is reliable.

The bottom line of it all is that no matter the expression, the equation will always balance.

The irony of it all is that the Universe has very few universal languages.

The most universal of all, not in word form but spoken brilliantly in the science of mathematics.

Angles, shapes, patterns.

Malleable perspective.

The addition and subtraction of Travelling Partners.

Divine symbols and signs.

We say it all the time, conditioned from our youth …

But just in case you need reminding: Humans seek safety.

In numbers.

Manifestation

Manifestation is sacred co-creation with the Universe.

You'll get exactly what you need, even if it's not *exactly* what you (think you) want.

Manifestation is The Balance Theory coming to fruition. Manifestation is cosmic communication with all that is.

Nothing more, nothing less.

Full
October 2020

My heart and my belly are both full.

I am currently seven months pregnant, very shortly going on

eight and ready to have babe enter earthside by early December.

Pregnancy—the beginning of this precious life—holds the lessons just as much and if not more than the process of conscious grieving.

This is the lesson of the *give in*. The beauty in surrender—the ability to suspend all physical, mental and emotional comforts in the name of universal trust.

Trust has been a recurring lesson for 2020. On a personal note, working through old patterns with my own coach, I've come to realise that we can have *toxic trust patterns* in the form of relying solely on ourselves. We often read articles in the conscious space on subjects like 'the art of saying no' and 'knowing when to ask for help', but we often do very little practical reflection on these ideals, let alone apply the principles. And while I could literally write the book on boundaries, self-confidence and self-empowerment, I have a lot of work to do in the realm of trust.

Trust beyond Self.

When you're growing a human life, you are hyper-aware that you can *do all the things*—treat the body as a temple, be conscious of your food, your thoughts, your sleep and your emotions, your patterns of consumption—but ultimately, your lesson is the coexistence, the co-creative power you hold with Source.

Pregnancy is a symbiotic and constant triad between Mother, Baby and Source—each party with their own intent, yet the energetics pull together in the sacred act of birth.

The birthing process holds a parallel train track with the

creative process.

By nature, human beings are inherently creative. We are all creative people. The fact that we have been given the capacity to reproduce is evidence for this sacred gift. In this way, our bodies are the canvas and they house the artist's ever-living potential. The art of creating a child—the pure joy that exists in the form of sex—is the expression of the *flow* state. The creative ease. This is our conversation with the Universe. We set the intention to create and Source provides the DNA—the means to the end. The sperm is perfectly balanced against the egg to duplicate the appropriate amount of cells to create the embryo.

The body just *does* this. The unconscious nature of conception is mind-bafflingly flawless. The genetic recipe is pre-written for each being: a specific and purpose-driven download.

It's magic, mysterious and an utterly marvellous balancing act until full gestation occurs and the cycle begins again.

New.

Born.

Day of the dead

The date was definitely not 2 November, but it might as well have been.

I sat at my desk; the management team who held their meetings in the centre of my office space were chit-chatting the morning away. Rapid speech caught my ears as discussions were had before the 8:00 am rush. Whose child had started a new day care and which cake to eat during morning tea seemed particularly insignificant that day.

Intuitively, I was channelling a hunch again. The day was already feeling different despite the same morning routine playing out with predictable precision behind me.

The ward on level four was waiting for me again. I was chowing down a banana and sipping a latte while replying to emails. I was also planning my exit route from the morning meeting with sharp strategy. I looked at my patient list. Five people to see after the doctors finished their rounds.

My manager called to me as I scurried down the hall to ensure my pager was charged. I was to be on alert for new referrals coming in from ED. The number five on the list would likely double before lunchtime.

I breathed in, hit the neon four on the lift and exhaled long and hard while I took the ride up to my level.

Acute clinical work was always a mental gearshift away from whatever was happening on the ground floor and the outside world. I changed gears, just in time, as the doors opened.

The pager went off. My patient on the floor below was in urgent need of a review, according to the short and punchy digital imprint on the pager screen. Level-four patients would have to wait.

Down I went, the course of the day about to unfold.

I reached the nurses station to be greeted by Pamela, a friendly nurse who just *knew* everything that went on behind the curtains. From patient stories to staff affairs, Pamela was your 'go to' hospital info centre for everything irrelevant to medical proceedings.

'I'm here for bed forty-six. Mr Harvey. While I'm here, I'll review Mr Ansley too.'

Pamela looked up from behind the computer and gave me the look. It's the look that nurses usually give after just having received the updates post rounds. The look that comes with having to change the whole day to suit 'doctor's orders'.

'Oh love, didn't you see the note? Mr Ansley, he just passed. Deteriorated overnight … family just left.'

'Thanks for letting me know, Pam. I'll document too.'

I always found it interesting that *RIP* was a sufficient note to make in a patient's file after they had passed. In a weird way, I found it almost endearing that something so commonplace and colloquial could be considered 'acceptable' in clinical files.

While documenting my own account of Mr Ansley's death in his file, I completed my ritual for patients passed, as per usual, at my desk. Consciously, I recalled his face; soft around the edges with a contrastingly pointy nose. I sent him godspeed and pictured him at peace as he crossed over. This thought process was interrupted quickly by a striking visual oppositional to the intention—the image of Mr Ansley's face, lifeless and cold, as his body was wheeled into a cab in the morgue. I brushed over that part mentally and came back to the present, just as the goosebumps raised on my skin.

The intuitive sign that the crossover had commenced.

As the shiver met my spine, I stared over at the empty bed from behind the nurses station. I gawked in amazement at just how fast a new face appeared in the same room, only minutes after speaking to Pam.

Bodies dissolve into beds until they are either sent home for bed rest or make peace with eternal rest.

I checked my list again. Back to level four.

Orderlies, doctors on phones, nurses attending to more pages. Nothing out of the ordinary.

Opposite every nurses station was the journey board. The board that coordinates the entire wing. I reviewed my patients—

Bed sixteen—RIP.

Bed thirty-two—RIP.

Bed forty-one—RIP.

My eyes darted left to right, up and down.

I checked and then triple checked.

Not one of my patients are alive today.

Even in a clinical setting that sees as much death as it does birth, that day felt particularly eerie.

The final one on my list was bed fifty, Mr Darmouth. End of the hall.

Perhaps just one interaction before midday, I reasoned to myself.

I reached the door that was slightly ajar, applied sanitiser, pulled a mask over my mouth and called out to introduce myself.

Immediately, a woman in her thirties emerged. Eyes swollen

from too much crying.

'Haven't you been told? My father passed away. Ten minutes ago. We won't be needing your service.'

She didn't lock eye contact. Her shoulders hung and collapsed into the rest of her body.

'I'm so sorry. My condolences.'

There was nothing more that I could say.

Some random date in May marked my own personal All Souls' Day.

I'll never know why 'all souls' on my list that day were called to their rest together, but I concluded that perhaps they were, in some way, Travelling Partners.

The thought made me smile in acceptance. It allowed me to continue my day with just the right amount of emotional reverence, professionalism still intact.

My patients—

Human strangers.

But spirit family.

———•———

By the time I returned for lunch, my senior supervisor checked in.

'There is a mass of referrals expected after lunch. ED is on another level today. How was the morning? I saw your list—you had a few to get through.'

'It was … peaceful.' I smiled as I slid into my chair to

complete the obligatory paperwork. The afternoon could be as busy as it wanted to be. It was the least of my concerns.

Death resolves human chaos, I figured.

The goosebumps rose again.

I rubbed my arms and got back to work.

Divine intervention
June 1991

Sandra was one of my first examples of unconditional love. If we're getting specific about the ancestral ties, we were cousins. Twice removed but really, she and I had travelled long before this lifetime.

The day I was born, she was having major surgery. Jaw reconstruction post traumatic car accident.

When she woke up in recovery, she turned to her sister, Annette, and said, 'How's Natasha?'

Annette cracked a half smile and reasoned she must be off her face from the post-surgical comedown.

'What are you talking about, mate?'

Sandra went on, fading. Eyes rolling.

'Call your cousin Frank. He's just had a baby girl. Her name's Natasha. I saw her birth. I was with Grace the whole time … she has a lot of hair.'

Annette sighed but went out into the hallway on the ground floor of the hospital to find the payphone.

Frank and Annette spoke.

Disbelief.

Annette hung up and walked back to Sandra's bedside, scratching her head.

'How did you *know*?'

'Just did. I was there. Soul-left-body stuff, you know ... we crossed over.'

To this day, Frank and Annette have no idea what truly happened in those hours that I was born and Sandra was in surgery but they have accepted Sandra was, in some way, particularly *special*.

January 2020

I wiped the dust off Sandra's picture resting on my lounge room mantelpiece.

The frame was white.

So was her dress. It gave off an angelic glow. I wondered if she looked that glamorous wherever she was resting.

Of course she did; she was stunning.

I checked my watch. I had twenty minutes to prepare my file.

The referral had come through only twenty-four hours prior. A priest needed his voice reviewed. Potential for nodules—and he had a funeral to service in two days. I smiled solemnly. I, too, would be attending a funeral in two days' time.

I was almost going to cancel the appointment.

Grief was creeping through my breath again. I didn't know how I was going to keep my voice strong. But then I thought of the poor family who would be burying a loved one and that gave me all the strength I needed to pull myself together for a forty-five-minute timeslot. This humble man needed his voice.

I wasn't sure where the man lived, but he opted for his session in my home clinic. Over the years, my lounge room and hallway passage had doubled as a waiting room once a week, on Tuesdays.

I prepped my voice and cleared the space.

The doorbell and the scuffle of shoes. He had arrived.

'Hi, Natasha. Thank you for seeing me on such late notice.'

'Not a problem, Father. Come on in.'

My years of Catholic school discipline overtook me and in that moment, I almost felt compelled to bless the man.

He handed me his referral paperwork; he had barely even entered the door yet.

'I've had a few voice problems on and off for a while now. But I really need some basic strategies to at least get through this funeral coming up. We can do the deeper work next week—I know there is something there to be looked at.'

'Sure, sure,' I assured him, gesturing with a smile for him to come through.

'The family of this woman is big. Beautiful, but there is a lot going on. She was young. Cancer. Another, gone too soon …'

He trailed off. I could see the attention in his eyes had shifted focus.

To something on my mantelpiece.

'I'm sorry,' he said, 'but do you mind if I ask—the woman in your photo ... she looks an awful lot like the lady that passed away.'

The pieces fell into place instantaneously.

The priest before me was going to be servicing *my* family.

I felt the gratitude, the pain, the sadness and the irony all at once. In the pit of my stomach; encroaching my heart space.

The Balance Theory, in real time. Again.

'Come on in, Father,' I repeated as I wiped a single tear from my cheek.

January 2012

'How's Vincent holding up, Tash?'

It was two weeks after Dylan's funeral. I was seated at Sandra's perfect table. We shared a pot of tea—white with two sugars each. Sandra always used the best china, no matter the occasion.

Pure indulgence is white tea, two sugars.

Sandra had an effortless way of making afternoon tea reverent. A dozen scones and a spotted plate to match the pattern on the china teacups.

'He's getting there. Day at a time,' I said tiredly.

'I just can't even imagine how his family are dealing with it all. My heart is broken. So young, gone too soon ... one of my friend's colleagues works with his mother ...'

I took her words in, scenes of the funeral flashing through my mind. Throwing red roses over Dylan's grave. Red against black felt particularly confronting that day. It was too striking.

'Sometimes, darling, when it's your time, it's your time, right?' she said with certainty.

I nodded in agreement, because ultimately it was true.

In her kitchen, eight years before we would be saying that about her, I knew that she, on some level, had come to accept how this crazy universe works.

The day that Sandra passed, I had called Mitch on my way home from work. We were working through 'pre-grief' over the phone.

I did grief differently with Sandra. It was conscious; a conscious farewell for my Travelling Partner. Before her decline and final hospitalisation, I had had a chance to tell her I loved her and that we would meet again in the next life. I was recounting said details to Mitch in an attempt to process it all, before I had to *process it all*.

We were wrapping up the conversation, Mitch telling me all the things that I needed to hear at that moment—that he would be there for me when 'it' happens. That whatever I needed, all I had to do was sing out.

'... I feel like when I go inside, I'm going to get news,' I ended.

'I got you,' he confirmed.

I got you.

Our favourite line.

At the time, I was consciously trying to conceive for the first time. Consequently, my diet was full of restrictions—my body was in full-blown 'spring cleaning' mode. Making all the space for babe to land.

No gluten, no dairy. No sugar. I hadn't touched anything in these categories for months.

I pulled up to my parents' house to be with my family. My dad, in particular, was doing it tough. He looked up to Sandra. They were close.

'Long day?' Mum started.

'You know, it was, but all is okay.'

I looked over to Jo and Sam. Jo looked drained. She went over to the cupboard.

'Tea, Tash? We've got everything and anything. Any flower you could imagine, in any combination. Herbal, right?'

I took a minute to check in with my body.

She was trying to tell me something.

'I'll have peppermint, thanks, Jo.'

'Are you sure?'

I wasn't.

'You know what? Actually, f*ck it. I'll have a *proper* tea. White tea—'

'Two sugars,' Jo finished, smiling gently.

My aunty appeared from behind the door.

Eyes swollen from too much crying.

'She's gone.'

I processed her words and became aware of my goosebumps.

The sign of the crossover.

I sipped my tea. Two sips. One shallow, choked with tears. The other, deep and indulgent. For Sandra.
Finally.
Peace.

The Balance Theory is such;
The science of life;
The divinity of it too.
Divine timing.
Divine encounters.
Divine succession of events.
Divine signs.
Divine symbols.
Divine systems.
Divine human.
Divine spirit.
Divine Masculine.
Divine Feminine.
If we surrender to that,
Unquestioning trust is the only outcome.
Reverence for death,
Reverence for life.
Unquestioning trust is yours to claim.
Your calm, your centre.
Inner peace.

Spirituality has no baseline.
Its science comes from a state of being.

Fully observed and measured.

Womb wisdom

Early on in my pregnancy, I had a vivid dream.

Lucid dreams are not uncommon for a woman pregnant.

During pregnancy, a woman's mind is just as pregnant with intuition as her womb is with life.

It was a simple dream.

Mitch and I were holding hands. Staring deadpan at the camera in my mind's eye.

Like a pop-punk album cover from the mid-noughties.

He was crying, and so was I.

My tears, happiness with a subtext of fear.

His, sadness.

I was heavily pregnant in the dream. The baby could have been birthed there and then.

That was it. We weren't in any particular place, as such. The art director in my dream space allowed for a white backdrop.

Ambiguous and vague.

Our emotions were the only sure thing about the dream.

When I woke the next morning, I knew—

Before the nausea set in and the phone call was had—

I would be giving birth in exchange for a loss of life.

The season would be Sagittarian.

The last dregs of November were set to be drowned out by the encroaching festive noise.

The birthdates would align.

And went like that—

It did.

The wedding invitation

Two days before our wedding, Vincent and I had a lovers' spat. Definitely not in the 'cold feet' category but enough to know that we needed to 'kiss and make up' before walking the aisle.

We had just bought our first home. We were hastily attempting to renovate, *The Block* style, before the big day, because why not renovate a house and get married in the same week?

We had our first dance playing on repeat in our soon-to-be living room, Michael Hutchence's lyrics sung by an emerging indie artist looping over and over in the background. No furniture, just sawdust and rusted paintbrushes creating trip hazards left, right and centre. We'd complete a few brushstrokes, fumble a dance practice in the mix because we were both determined to 'get it right', and then continue with the quarrel. It was a weird vibe but we were comfortable with being uncomfortable with each other after nine years. This went on for hours.

I honestly can't even remember the source of the argument. Tensions were running high; it was probably about the texture of the kitchen splashback but it also probably wasn't about that at all.

We left our home with one thing one hundred per cent decided upon. We were both disappointed that neither of us had visited Dylan's grave to invite him to the wedding. It had been something so important on the final to-do list that week—and yet, here we were, nearly thirty hours to go—and no space to go to the cemetery.

We both accepted defeat, begrudgingly, and parted. He drove left and I, right. We agreed we loved each other and that we'd meet at the aisle. It was less than ideal.

I calculated my time and told my mum I had something to 'take care of'. I was extremely calm and clear. I also knew that I didn't want to be home at lunchtime, the day before my wedding.

My final chance for true 'alone' time. I seized the opportunity.

After promising her that I was definitely fine and that she wouldn't have to send out a search party, I took off. Started the car and just drove.

I took it upon myself to take a spare wedding invite to lay at Dylan's grave. It would be part of my wedding gift to Vincent. As he was living on the other side of Sydney, there was no way he'd be able to get there in a timely fashion. Vincent doesn't do 'timely'. I knew better than that.

I arrived thirty minutes later.

I walked over to his headstone—positioned under a

gorgeous tree casting a shadow in the afternoon glow. The sun filtered perfectly through the leaves. The peace was palpable.

I had my moment and left the invite.

I was sad that he wouldn't be standing next to us when we said our vows. I told him that.

I heard his voice. Loud, clear, booming with laughter through a smile so perfect it would bring Hollywood shame.

'If you two get together,' Dylan had said to us both during our final school days, seven years earlier, 'you'll end up married. There will be no in-between.'

His prophecy was about to be realised.

He was with me. I felt him all around.

I was satisfied.

I left.

I was ten minutes from home.

Processing it all.

Listening to all the right songs to cradle me in the feels.

A flash zipped past me as I raced past the 80km sign.

There and then, I spun the wheel, stopping only briefly to consider oncoming traffic, and sped ridiculously in the complete opposite direction.

I knew the sound of the car before I saw it and saw him.

Vincent.

I have no idea how the hell we ended up on the same road

without a single conversation. If we had planned it—it wouldn't have happened. I tailgated him all the way back to the cemetery. He caught my eyes in his rear-view mirror.

I could see him observing my tears. We laughed and choked up together.

Over Dylan's grave, Vincent and I made our formal invite.

We made our vows for life, with Dylan officiating, before the hundreds of guests would bear witness the next day.

A Travelling Partner commits for lifetimes.
They are the gatekeepers for our memories.
Whether on this earth or beyond,
Trust that the invitation will always arise.
The vows will exchange in the form of loving energy.
Never in timely fashion,
Not always convenient.
But rest assured,
Kismet.

Trust that the surrender you feel, so human and raw, is orchestrated with—

Energy from here, *being directed* there.
Through words, action, intention and happenstance—
Leading you exactly where you need to be.

All is inherently good.

Aum

It is said that at the time *it all began*, the Universe made one, single primordial sound.
/Aum/.
The way that it resounds through the aether vibrates at the frequency of healing. The sound shape shifts in perfect harmony, bringing the articulators—teeth, tongue and lips—to rest while the throat opens to channel the healthiest form of verbal expression.

It was no surprise to me when I learned as a student that clinically, if we were to treat tension in the vocal folds, the vibration of /aum/ creates quintessential, rhythmic waves. The touchpoints between the folds, when met with adequate breath work, have the capacity to produce clarity of tone and relieve muscle tension in the vocal tract.

The sound is a reflection of human surrender and safety.
Of authentic expression.
For my son, the sound of /aum/ in his ear calms him right into a state of peace, especially when at the height of overwhelm. It is the sound of love; of metaphysical safety.

And that's why, in the form of phonetic transcription, /aum/

is literally tattooed onto my right ribcage.

It was my touchpoint through labour.

It is my constant, physical reminder that I will always have breath when all else fails. Proof that as long as there is breath, there is life.

A reminder that at the end of it all—

It begins with the same sound.

We are round and we are whole.

Because the Universe's only goal is to experience balance.

Pneuma—

Rising and falling.

As per the Universal laws that govern it.

We live it, we breathe it.

We are it.

The lesson

At the end of it all, is the beginning.

Life is death.

And back again.

Rebirth and death are one and the same.

You know you've got life 'figured out' when you realise life will never be 'figured out'.

Search far and wide, and every corner of the Universe will teach you the same lesson—

Connection to Self, Other and the world is kismet.

At whatever level you observe, with whichever lens you've been dealt, all the Universe has ever wanted is to experience the process of homeostasis.

Of rightful energy exchange.

One in, one out.

This for *that*.

From the cellular to the cosmic.

From quantum theory to the big bang.

A constant, relentless and unapologetic game.

The Balance Theory.

Questions for your soul work

1

The Balance Theory speaks to one Universal goal—the Universe is simply attempting to experience itself via means of balance and rebalance. At the end of this journey, how does this statement feel for you?

2

How has The Balance Theory manifested in your life? I encourage you to go and recap 'The lesson' from each chapter as you reflect on your answer.

Notes

1   Source: 2020, The Black Dog Institute, www.blackdoginstitute.org.au/resources-support/depression

2   Published in 2016, our research proposed that close to thirty per cent of young people aged eighteen to twenty-four experience a clinically diagnosed mental health condition. *Full citation:* Natasha M Perre, Nathan J Wilson, Jennifer Smith-Merry, and Gillian Murphy. 2016. 'Australian University Students' Perceptions of Mental Illness: A Qualitative Study.' *Journal of the Australian and New Zealand Student Services Association: Number 48*: 1–13

3   Final—for now. I am very aware that mental health issues can often 'flare up' based on the situation. I am not so naïve as to think that in my lifetime, I will probably need to re-engage with mental health services. This is the nature of lived mental illness.

4   I want to be very clear here; I am not condoning this at all. Some states of mental illness require medication to help with functioning. Some people have their lives depend on it on a daily basis and hence medication is crucial. The medication acts as the mediator, helping the individual to experience homeostasis from a chemical point of view. Medication can be one-hundred-per-cent necessary for many people.

Perhaps it was intuition, stubbornness or a combination of both, but I knew medication was not my route to health.

For what it's worth, this is simply a sharing of my story, and yours may look different. If medication is true for you—absolutely engage with it under the careful guidance of your medical professional. Your mind, body and soul will thank you in the long run.

At the time, medication was simply not my truth and I worked through this under the directive of my medical and mental health professionals.

5   CBT is a commonly known and practised psychological therapy known as 'cognitive behavioural therapy'.

6   Sensory processing is defined as the way a person perceives, processes and organises the information that they receive through their senses such as hearing, sight, touch, smell, taste and movement. This sensory information comes from your own body and the environment around you.
www.autismspectrum.org.au > Fact sheets > *Sensory Processing*

7   REM sleep is rapid-eye-movement sleep—the part of the sleep cycle where most of our dreaming occurs.

Acknowledgements

Writing the acknowledgements at the end of this book really was an important part of the process. *The Balance Theory*, formed via many Travelling Partner stories and conversations over the years that have held such significance in my life, deserves serious contemplation when it comes to acknowledgements. Here we go.

Alfie: My beautiful boy. My sonshine. My whole heart. Mama tried to finish this book about three times over the past ten years. And of course, it could not be done until you fell into physical existence. To write about the balance that is birthed through the life/death cycle, I needed to experience rebirth in the shape of you.

I am forever grateful for you. I love you. You taught me more than you'll ever know before you were even conceived. I was waiting for you to birth my creative fire. You made this happen. Thank you.

Vincent: The way we hold each other is unmatched. We've been travelling for lifetimes now. I'd choose you every time. We knew, from that first awkwardly forced seating arrangement in class, we'd be together forever. Your support for this book and my entire life perspective is so incredible. Co-creating this life with you is my favourite pastime. I love you.

My dear Publisher: To Natasha Gilmour and the kind press team, it was divine timing indeed. Thank you for believing in me and the lessons of *The Balance Theory*. We said it all along: this process was sacred co-creation. I'm blessed to have had the amazing experience that I did, as a first-time author. To my wonderful editor, Georgia Jordan, your professionalism and respect for this concept was profoundly next level. Thank you for offering your time and unique perspective. Eternal gratitude to you.

To Mum and Dad Perre: Thank you for your unconditional love and support. It has never wavered. I had always told you that I would write a book. Thank you for supporting the dream of that little girl. Here we are. I've written a book about the lessons of life that you've gifted me. Thank you endlessly.

To Mum and Dad Piccolo: Your love and guidance are stellar. This book would not have happened without your support. Thank you for loving me like your own.

To my grandparents: Thank you for teaching me that sacrifice is well worth it. You are all so special.

To Nat and Jo: You have always seen me. You have always heard me. I will love you both forever.

To Lewis, Sam, Michael and Rochelle: Life is joyous because you exist.

To Theo: You are the definition of limitless love.

To my aunties, uncles, cousins and the Small family: You make my life rich. Every encounter is my backbone. Thank you. A special mention to Uncle Fred and Aunty Anna, my first spirit guides.

To Mitch: There are not enough words to express my love and gratitude for you. I thank you and Tanya for allowing me to share your story and for granting me permission to honour Dalton's memory in this book. Let's just keep travelling together. So much of this book is you. Life lessons with you are my absolute favourite. Universe gave me more than a soul brother when it gifted you. To this lifetime, and the next and the next ...

To Alex, Mel, Sam: When we are together, magic happens. We are more than best friends and perhaps even Travelling Partners. Let's be one another's cheerleaders forever. There are not many memories in life that don't include you all. That says it all.

To Lucy: This book exists because you gave me the space to explore an untapped corner of my mind. I will never be able to thank you enough for the way you've shaped my world view. Endless love and gratitude for our friendship and all the lessons that you and Beau have taught me.

To Kirsty: My soul sister. You absolutely get me. I am so lucky to have you to travel with in this lifetime. Thank you for your endless love and support. From work to books to babies and all that is in between—I can't wait to see what we do next together.

To Joe: The time and effort you invested into my process will never be forgotten. I appreciate you so much. Thank you.

To my brain's trust and especially Joey, Nicole, Maz, Thep,

Lil, Liz and Kirralee: Every memory, every conversation, every phone call, every check-in, every moment spent with you is Heaven on Earth. You each have a piece of my heart.

To Jordanna Levin: Thank you for believing in me and this concept. Because of you, *The Balance Theory* turned into a physical book for the rest of the world to enjoy. I respect and value every mentoring session we had on this journey. I can't thank you enough.

To the design team, Nikki Jane and Mila: You brought this vision to visualisation. Your work is stunning. Thank you.

To my clients: To all my clients. Past, present and future. You are my eternal motivation. You have been heard. You have shaped me. Giving you your voice is my life's mission. To Ave, thank you for allowing me to share your story. You inspire me every single day. To Aiden, thank you for teaching me that not all voices need to be spoken to be heard.

To my Travelling Partners beyond our Earth space, especially Dylan, Sandra, Chiara and Aunty Tracey: You are my teachers, my guides, my complete belief in Universal guidance. You are The Balance Theory. I will forever cherish you.

To Caf: Thank you for your blessing in allowing me to share Dylan's name and story. His memory will never be forgotten.

To my earthside Travelling Partners: Every single one of you. You know who you are. You have each made my life story a *life story*. Thank you for giving me permission to share our stories. I'm sure we will be choosing each other for lifetimes to come.

To my dear reader: Universal guidance landed you here.

Trust that the lessons were always supposed to land, just as they are and just as they have.

    Best always,
    Tash.

About the author

Natasha Piccolo

Natasha Piccolo is a mama, small business owner and author who hopes to motivate others to live a life that is consciously aligned. In Natasha's personal and professional life, it is the magic in people's stories that inspire her most.

Natasha is always up for a good chat, with her main work roles including clinical speech pathology, and life coaching. Her business, Resonate Holistic, assists clients to facilitate healthy communication throughout their lives.

Natasha also runs a gelato cart events business, Pina Piccolina, with her husband. She appreciates the fullness, fun and fulfilment in her life. When she isn't singing her son nursery rhymes or working at the office, Natasha loves nothing more than a long brunch date, a juicy yoga sesh, delicious tea and a great book.

In The Balance Theory, Natasha shares a collection of teachings received over the course of a decade that pose the question: what if all the Universe wanted was to experience balance?

This I Know Is True: A collection of stories celebrating awakened women to inspire community progress (the kind press, 2021) is Natasha's first co-authored publication.

IG: @tashspeaks / @resonate_holistic
www.resonateholistic.com.au

www.ingramcontent.com/pod-product-compliance
Lightning Source LLC
Chambersburg PA
CBHW031238290426
44109CB00012B/345